Greeting Cards
for All Occasions

Written and Illustrated by
Jerome C. Brown

Fearon Teacher Aids

An imprint of Paramount Supplemental Education

Executive Editor: Carolea Williams
Editors: Kristin Eclov and Christine Hood
Cover Design: Dianne Platner
Inside Design: Terry McGrath

ISBN 0-86653-881-X

Printed in the United States of America

1. 9 8 7 6 5 4 3 2 1

Contents

Introduction 1
Directions for Making
    Folded Pop-Up Greeting Cards 2
Directions for Making
    Standing Pop-Up Greeting Cards 4

Fall

Citizenship Day (September 17) 5
Rosh Hashanah (September-October) 7
American Indian Day (4th Friday in September) 9
Halloween (October 31)
    Black Cat 11
    Scarecrow 13
    Pumpkin 15
Thanksgiving (4th Thursday in November)
    Pop-Up Turkey 17
    Holiday Harvest 19
    Turkey 21

Winter

Hanukkah (End of November-Early December) 23
Christmas (December 25)
    Holiday Tree 25
    Santa Claus 27
    Feast of Saint Nicholas 30
    Stockings 33
    Snowman 35
    Recycled Greeting Cards 37
    Make Your Own Envelope 38
    Decorate Your Envelope 39
Kwanzaa (December 26-January 1) 41
New Years Day (January 1) 44
Martin Luther King, Jr. Birthday (January 15) 46
Winter Cheer
    Flip-Top Snowperson 48
    Mittens 50
Chinese New Year (January 21-February 19) 52

Valentine's Day (February 14)
    Valentine Bee 54
    Valentine Dog 56
    Valentine Frog 58
Presidents' Day (3rd Monday in February)
    Washington 60
    Lincoln 62

Spring
St. Patrick's Day (March 17)
    Shamrock 64
    Leprechaun 66
Eid (Muslim, celebrated twice a year) 68
Easter (March-April)
    Easter Eggs 70
    Circle Bunny 72
    Spring Chick 74
Earth Day (April 22) 76
May Day (May 1) 78
Children's Day (May 5) 80
Cinco de Mayo (May 5)
    Boy 82
    Girl 84
Mother's Day (May 8)
    Flower Basket 86
    Flowerpot 88

**Summer/
Miscellaneous**
Father's Day (June 19)
    BBQ 90
    Newspaper 93
Canada Day (July 1) 95
U.S. Independence Day (July 4)
    Bald Eagle 97
    Liberty Bell 99
Birthday
    Jack-in-the-Box 101
    Cupcake 103
School Events
    Apple 105
    School House 107

Introduction

Greeting Cards for All Occasions contains reproducible activity sheets for making cards that are fun, easy, and inexpensive. Each activity provides a tidbit of information about the holiday or symbol, instructions, and patterns for making the greeting card. The patterns can be easily adapted to meet the individual needs of your students.

Organizational Helps

Construction paper is used for each greeting card. It is referred to as art paper in the list of materials that accompanies each project. Colors of art paper are suggested but can be changed to suit your needs. The term *skin tone* is used instead of a particular color of art paper for cards featuring people. Since a pencil, ruler, scissors, glue, markers, or crayons, and black felt pen are needed for most greeting cards, these items are not listed in each materials list.

Special instruction sheets for making different kinds of pop-up cards have been included at the beginning of this book. Once students have mastered the basic format, each card will take less time and explanation. Half sheets [9" x 12" (22.9 cm x 30.5 cm)] and quarter sheets [6" x 9" (15.2 cm x 22.9 cm)] of art paper are used whenever possible to cut down on the time spent measuring and cutting.

Before beginning each card, reproduce a pattern sheet for each student. Have students cut out all pieces so they can be used for tracing on the colored art paper. For younger children, patterns (which are not cut on a fold line) can be reproduced on white art paper. Color the patterns with markers or crayons and cut them out. This will eliminate the extra steps of tracing and cutting a second time.

Folded Pop-Up Greeting Cards

Greeting cards are made with a 9" x 12"
(22.9 cm x 30.5 cm) piece of art paper.

Fold 9" x 12" (22.9 cm x 30.5 cm)
art paper into 9" x 6" (22.9 cm
x 15.2 cm). Cut two slits 1 1/2"
(3.9 cm) long and 2" (5.0 cm)
apart on the fold.

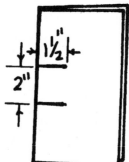

Fold the piece between the slits
away from the fold.

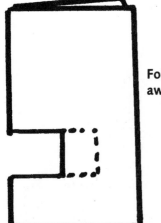

Open the paper and fold slit
piece in the opposite direction of
the fold. The slit piece should
pop up when the card is opened.

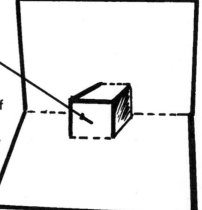

GLUE PUMPKIN
HERE

Glue the pattern to the front of
the slit piece.

Finish the folded pop-up card following
the directions on the activity page.

2

Vertical Folded Pop-Up Greeting Cards

Greeting cards are made with a 9" x 12" (22.9 cm x 30.5 cm) piece of art paper.

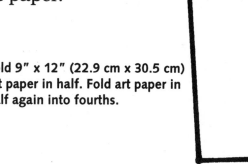

Fold 9" x 12" (22.9 cm x 30.5 cm) art paper in half. Fold art paper in half again into fourths.

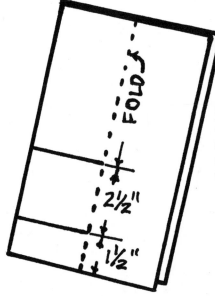

Unfold and cut two slits on folded edge down to fold line. One slit should be 1 1/2" (3. 9 cm) and the other slit should be 4" (10.2 cm) from the edge of the paper.

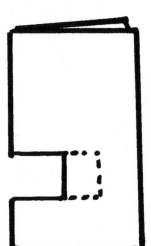

Fold the piece between the slits away from the fold.

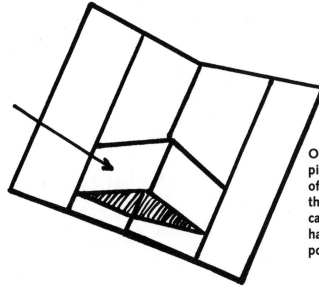

Open the paper and fold slit piece in the opposite direction of the fold. The piece between the slits should pop up when the card is opened. Fold pattern in half and glue to the fold of the pop-up piece.

Directions for Making
Standing Pop-Up Greeting Cards

Greeting cards are made with a 9" x 12" (22.9 cm x 30.5 cm) piece of art paper.

Fold art paper with design in half making a crease. Then make creases on the dotted lines. Fold the figure forward on the dotted lines so that the figure is inside the card.

Open the paper and the figure should pop out.

HOLiDAY

GREETiNGS

Greeting Cards for All Occasions ©1995 Fearon Teacher Aids

Citizenship Day

Celebrated on the anniversary of the signing of the U.S. Constitution. Citizenship Day is set aside to honor new citizens of the United States, their common immigrant background, and the joy of citizenship. Ask students if they know where their ancestors are from.

Materials

Patterns on page 6
Art Paper:
    White 9" x 12" (22.9 cm x 30.5 cm)
    Skin tone 9" x 12"
      (22.9 cm x 30.5 cm)
    Blue 2" x 9" (5.0 cm x 22.9 cm)
    Red 2 1/2" x 9" (6 cm x 22.9 cm)
American flag on toothpick

Procedure

1. Fold skin tone 9" x 12" (22.9 cm x 30.5 cm) art paper in half, horizontally. Trace outline of boy or girl on the center fold of skin tone paper.
2. Use a black felt pen to trace around the pattern.
3. Add details to the boy or girl with markers or crayons.
4. Measure 4 3/4" (12.1 cm) from the bottom of the skin tone paper. Lightly draw a pencil line from the edge of the paper to the design. Do not draw on the figure.
5. Carefully cut along the line to the design, around the design, and continue cutting to the edge of the paper.
6. Follow directions on page 4 for making a standing pop-up card.
7. Glue cut out to folded white 9" x 12" (22.9 cm x 30.5 cm) art paper matching center folds.
8. Glue red, white, and blue stars as shown in Figure A on page 6.
9. Glue toothpick flag in figure's hand.
10. Use black felt pen for lettering or create your own message.

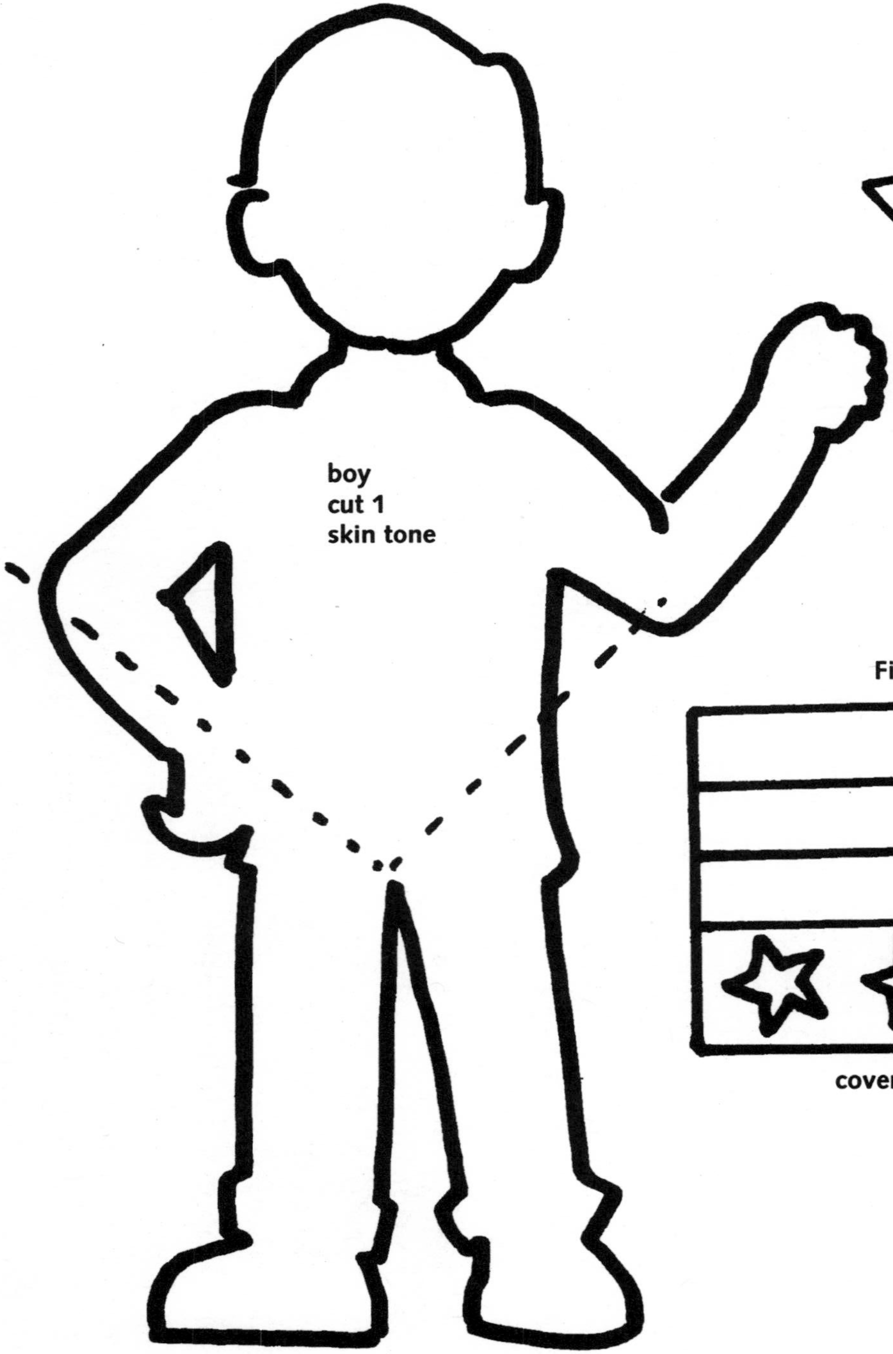

girl
cut 1
skin tone

star
cut 1 of each
red,
white,
blue

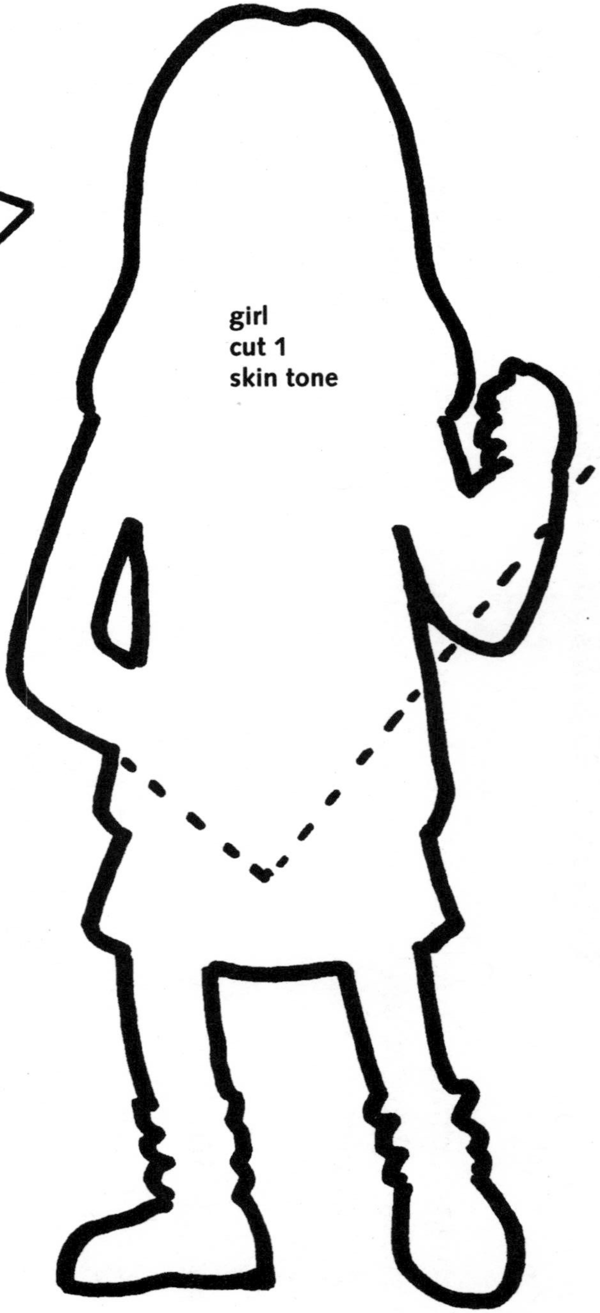

Figure A

cover of card

boy
cut 1
skin tone

Rosh Hashanah

Rosh Hashanah is celebrated the first two days of the Hebrew month of Tishri, which falls between September 5–October 5. Rosh Hashanah is the celebration of the Jewish New Year. The Jewish people celebrate their history and make promises for the new year. The most recognizable symbol of the Hebrew nation is the Star of David. It is formed from two interlaced triangles that form a six-pointed star.

Materials

Patterns on page 8
Art Paper:
    Light Blue 9" x 12" (22.9 cm x 30.5 cm)
    Purple 4 1/2" x 6" (11.4 cm x 15.2 cm)
Gold star

Figure A

Procedure

1. Fold 9" x 12" (22.9 cm x 30.5 cm) light blue art paper in half.
2. Using a purple marker, draw a line 1" (2.5 cm) from the edge of the folded paper. Then draw another line 1/4" (6 mm) from the previous line. Repeat on the opposite side. See Figure A.
3. Trace star pattern on purple art paper.
4. Cut out the two part star and glue as shown in Figure A.
5. Glue gold star in center of light blue art paper.
6. Print greeting inside of card.

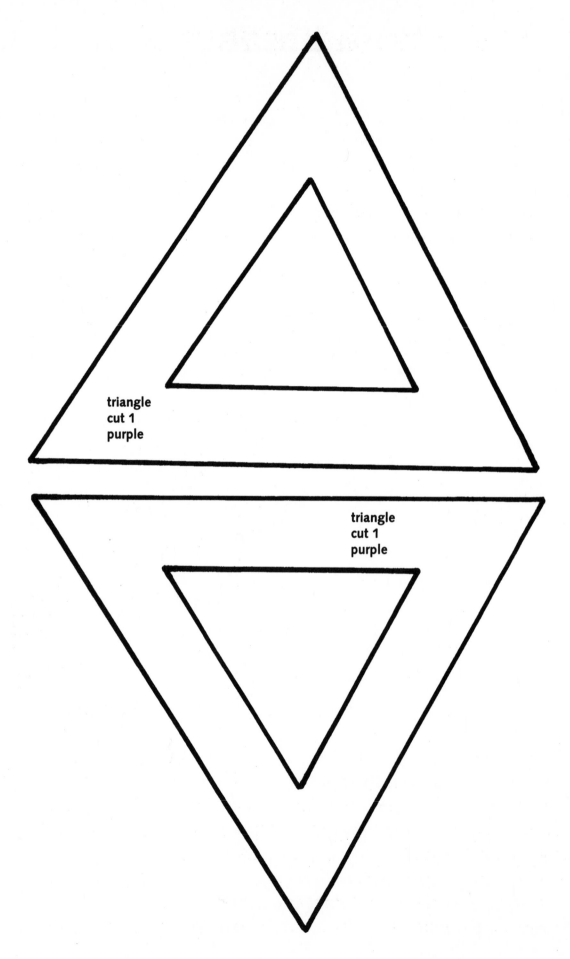

triangle
cut 1
purple

triangle
cut 1
purple

American Indian Day

Kachinas are sacred spirits representing many aspects of nature celebrated in dance and song. Ritual dances assuming the various "personalities" of the kachinas were often performed among the Hopi to reaffirm their bond with nature. These dances passed on generations of farming and ecological wisdom and tradition. This kachina is *Tawa*, who represents the spirit of the sun.

Materials

Patterns on page 10
Art Paper:
    Red 9" x 12"
       (22.9 cm x 30.5 cm)
    Yellow 6" x 9"
       (15.2 cm x 22.9 cm)

Procedure

1. Trace kachina pattern on yellow 6" x 9" (15.2 cm x 22.9 cm) art paper.
2. Outline pattern with black felt pen and color with crayons or markers. Cut out kachina pattern.
3. Trace, color, and outline the staff. Cut out a circle for the sun.
4. Follow directions on page 4 for making a standing pop-up card.
5. Glue kachina to folded red 9" x 12" (22.9 cm x 30.5 cm) art paper matching center folds.
6. Glue lower arms and lower body to create pop-up result.
7. Glue the sun in place and decorate the background of the card.

kachina
cut 1
yellow

staff
cut 1
yellow

Black Cat

Halloween is filled with legends and superstitions. Superstitions result from fears of the unknown. One common superstition is that bad luck will come to anyone whose path is crossed by a black cat. Cats are creatures of the night. They can see in the dark and often hunt at night. Superstition links black cats with darkness and mystery.

Materials

Patterns on page 12
Art Paper:
    Black 9" x 12"
      (22.9 cm x 30.5 cm)
    Orange 9" x 12"
      (22.9 cm x 30.5 cm)
    White scraps

Procedure

1. Fold orange and black 9" x 12" (22.9 cm x 30.5 cm) art paper in half.
2. Fold orange art paper in half again into fourths.
3. Follow directions on page 3 for making a vertical folded pop-up card.
4. Trace and cut out cat, ghosts, and bats.
5. Fold cat in half matching the cat to the fold of the slit and glue in place.
6. Glue ghosts and bats to the background.
7. Write a Halloween greeting with black felt pen.

bat
cut 2
black

ghost
cut 2
white

cat
cut 1
black

Scarecrow

Throughout history, Halloween has also been considered as a harvest festival celebrating the last days of summer and the coming of fall. One symbol of the harvest is the scarecrow. The scarecrow is often fashioned as a man stuffed with straw. Farmers mount scarecrows on poles among their crops, hoping that crows and other pests will be scared away.

Materials

Pattern on page 14
Art Paper:
    Orange 9" x 12"
      (22.9 cm x 30.5 cm)
    Yellow 9" x 12"
      (22.9 cm x 30.5 cm)
    Black scraps

Procedure:

1. Fold orange 9" x 12" (22.9 cm x 30.5 cm) art paper in half.
2. Reproduce scarecrow pattern on yellow 9" x 12" (22.9 cm x 30.5 cm) art paper.
3. Decorate with crayons or markers.
4. Carefully cut along the solid line from the edge of the paper, around the scarecrow, to the other edge of the paper.
5. Follow directions on page 4 for making a standing pop-up card.
6. Glue cut out to folded orange 9" x 12" (22.9 cm x 30.5 cm) art paper.
7. Match the folds for the scarecrow and the outside of the card before gluing. Then glue the design to the inside of the orange paper. Be careful not to glue the pop-up section of the card.
8. Cut out and glue bats to the orange background.
9. Write a Halloween greeting inside the card.

bat
cut 1
black

fold

fold

Pumpkin

One of the most popular Halloween traditions is carving pumpkins into jack-o'-lanterns. Jack-o'-lanterns are believed to have originated from an old Irish tale. In this story, a man named Jack hollowed out a turnip to use as a lantern. He placed a hot coal inside to light his way in the night. Originally, children of Ireland carved faces in turnips and potatoes and hollowed them to hold candles. Today, children carve pumpkins instead.

Materials

Patterns on page 16
Art Paper:
 Black 9" x 12"
 (22.9 cm x 30.5 cm)
 Orange 5" x 6"
 (12.7 cm x 15.2 cm)
 White 4" x 6"
 (10.2 cm x 15.2 cm)
 Yellow 3" x 3"
 (7.6 cm x 7.6 cm)

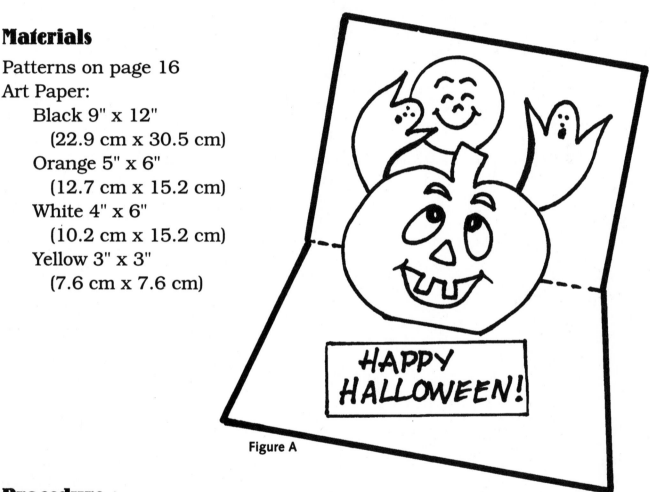

Figure A

Procedure

1. Fold black 9" x 12" (22.9 cm x 30.5 cm) art paper in half.
2. Follow directions on page 2 for making a folded pop-up card.
3. Cut out pumpkin, moon, and ghost.
4. Decorate patterns with crayons or markers.
5. Glue cut outs in place. See Figure A.
6. Write Halloween message on white 2" x 4" (5.0 cm x 10.2 cm) art paper with black felt pen. Glue message in place.

pumpkin
cut 1
orange

moon
cut 1
yellow

ghost
cut 2
white

Pop-Up Turkey

In 1620, pilgrims traveled to the United States from England in a ship called the Mayflower and founded the Plymouth Colony. Native Americans of the Wampanoag tribe taught the pilgrims how to plant corn and survive in the wilderness. The pilgrims invited the Native Americans to share in a Thanksgiving feast to celebrate their bountiful harvest. The first Thanksgiving meal consisted of ducks, geese, turkeys, fish, cornbread, leeks, and plums.

Materials

Pattern on page 18
Art Paper:
> Brown 9" x 12"
> (22.9 cm x 30.5 cm)
> White 8 1/2" x 11"
> (21 cm x 27 cm)

Procedure

1. Reproduce turkey pattern on white 8 1/2" x 11" (21 cm x 27 cm) art paper.
2. Use crayons or markers to add details.
3. Carefully cut along the solid line from the edge of the paper, around the turkey, to the other edge of the paper.
4. Follow directions on page 4 for making a standing pop-up card.
5. Fold 9" x 12" (22.9 cm x 30.5 cm) brown art paper in half.
6. Glue folded turkey to the brown background. The turkey should pop up when the card is opened.

Holiday Harvest

Otherwise known as "the horn of plenty," the cornucopia is the symbol of a full and bountiful harvest. The Thanksgiving cornucopia represents the abundance of everything we have to be thankful for. Ask students what things they are thankful for.

Materials

Patterns on page 20
Art Paper:
    White 9" x 12"
      (22.9 cm x 30.5 cm)
    Brown 9" x 12"
      (22.9 cm x 30.5 cm)
    Assorted scraps

Figure A

Procedure

1. Fold 9" x 12" (22.9 cm x 30.5 cm) white art paper in half.
2. Trace and cut out cornucopia using brown 9" x 12" (22.9 cm x 30.5 cm) art paper.
3. Follow the directions on page 2 for making folded pop-up cards.
4. Trace and cut out fruits and vegetables.
5. Glue fruits and vegetables to the front of the cornucopia. See Figure A.
6. Write holiday greetings on a torn piece of brown art paper and glue inside card.
7. Decorate background with crayons and scraps of paper.

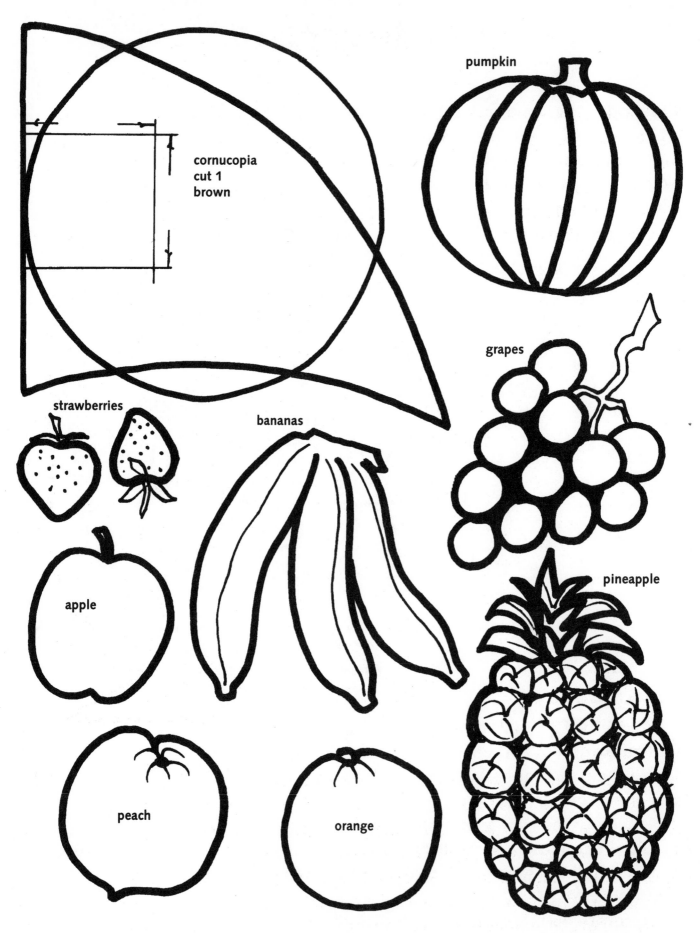

pumpkin

cornucopia
cut 1
brown

grapes

strawberries

bananas

apple

pineapple

peach

orange

Turkey

Long ago, turkeys were raised for food by the Native Americans and eventually became part of the traditional Thanksgiving dinner. Male turkeys, called *toms*, have a long, loose piece of skin called a *wattle* that extends from beneath their lower jaws along their necks. Some tom turkeys can weight up to 50 pounds! Many families serve turkey on Thanksgiving. Ask students if there are special foods served in their homes on Thanksgiving.

Materials

Pattern on page 22
Art Paper:
    Brown 9" x 12"
      (22.9 cm x 30.5 cm)
    Red 2" x 3"
      (5.0 cm x 7.6 cm)
    Black 3" x 6"
      (7.6 cm x 15.2 cm)
    White 2" x 4"
      (5.0 cm x 10.2 cm)
Hole punch

Procedure

1. Fold 9" x 12" (22.9 cm x 30.5 cm) brown art paper in half.
2. Trace and cut out turkey pattern on folded brown art paper.
3. Trace and cut out head and wing from turkey pattern.
4. Glue head and wing to folded turkey.
5. Use hole punch to make an eye. Glue eye in place.
6. Write Thanksgiving message on white 2" x 4" (5.0 cm x 10.2 cm) art paper. Glue message inside card.

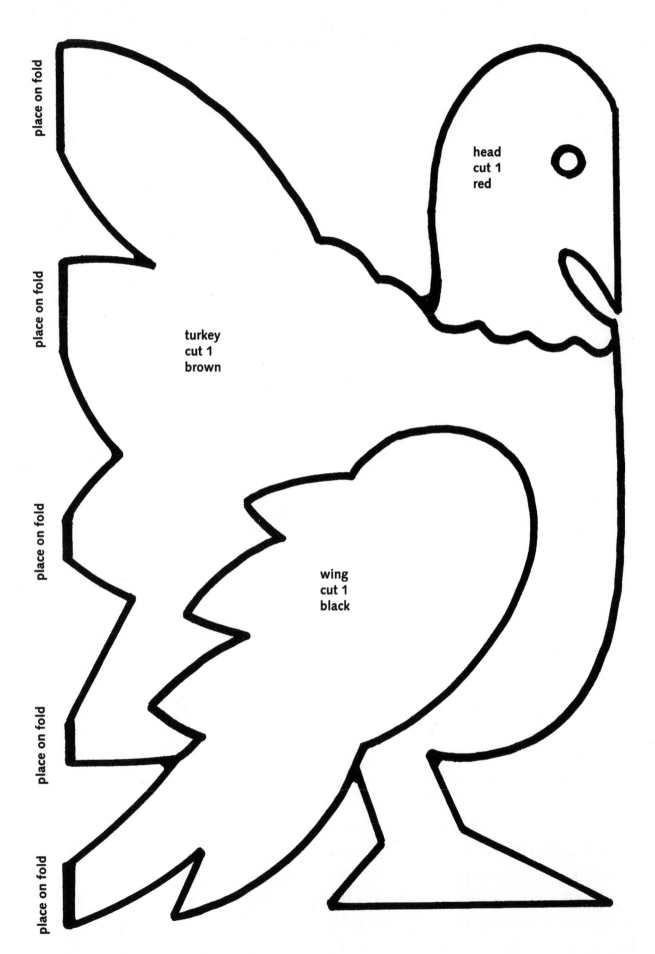

place on fold

place on fold

place on fold

place on fold

place on fold

head
cut 1
red

turkey
cut 1
brown

wing
cut 1
black

Hanukkah

The menorah is a traditional symbol of Judaism. It is a nine-branched candelabrum used during the holy days of Hanukkah. Every night during these eight days, Jewish families use the ninth candle (the shammash) to light one of the other eight, until on the last night, all the candles will be burning brightly. After the lighting of each candle, special meals and gifts are shared between family members.

Materials

Patterns on page 24
Art Paper:
- Purple 9" x 12" (22.9 cm x 30.5 cm)
- Turquoise 9" x 12" (22.9 cm x 30.5 cm)
- Orange 3" x 4" (7.6 cm x 10.2 cm)
- Blue 1" x 3" (2.5 cm x 7.6 cm)
- White 6" x 9" (15.2 cm x 22.9 cm)

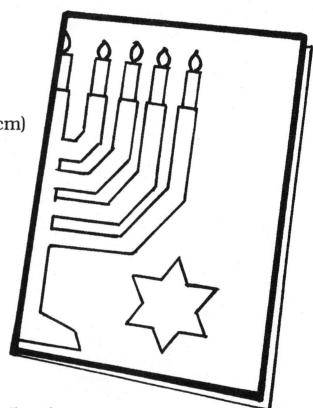

Procedure

1. Fold turquoise 9" x 12" (22.9 cm x 30.5 cm) art paper in half. Place menorah pattern on the fold.
2. Trace and cut out menorah.
3. Cut out eight white candles and one blue candle.
4. Cut out nine orange flames and one orange star.
5. Fold purple paper in half. Glue menorah on the outside of the fold.
6. Glue the blue candle in the center of the menorah, then glue four white candles on each side of the blue candle.
7. Glue the orange flames on each of the candles.
8. Glue the orange star to the cover of the card.
9. Write a Hanukkah greeting inside the card.

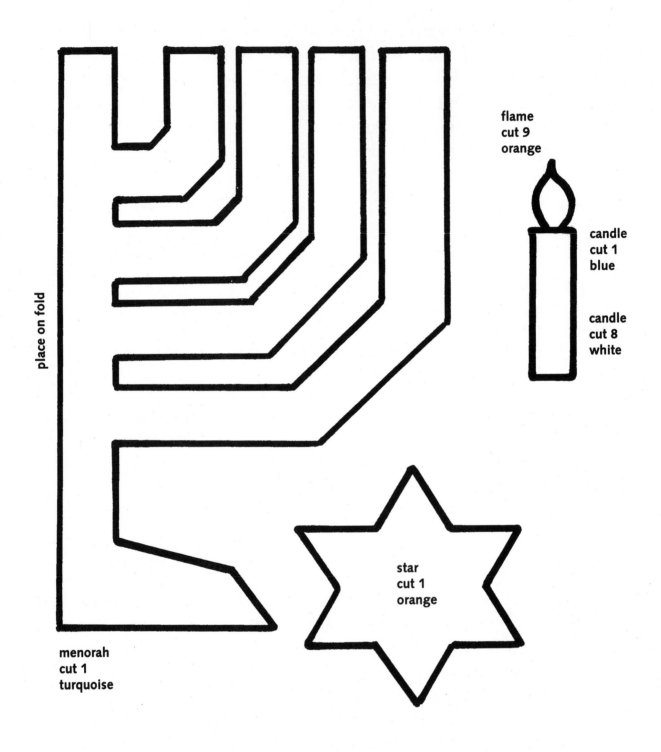

place on fold

flame
cut 9
orange

candle
cut 1
blue

candle
cut 8
white

menorah
cut 1
turquoise

star
cut 1
orange

Greeting Cards for All Occasions ©1995 Fearon Teacher Aids

Holiday Tree

The fir tree has long been considered as the wood of peace. Germany saw this tree as a sign of immortality because its leaves are ever green and its top branches point straight to heaven. It seems that the Germans brought the tradition of the Christmas tree to the United States. Why do we adorn our trees with lights and beads, tinsel, and bulbs? Some say it is to reflect the sparkling stars in the Christmas Eve sky.

Materials

Patterns on page 26
Art Paper:
    Red 9" x 12"
      (22.9 cm x 30.5 cm)
    White 6" x 9"
      (15.2 cm x 22.9 cm)
    Green 6" x 9"
      (15.2 cm x 22.9 cm)
    Assorted scraps
Stickers
Magazine pictures

Procedure

1. Trace and cut out tree on green 6" x 9" (15.2 cm x 22.9 cm) art paper.
2. Decorate tree with stickers, ornaments made from paper scraps, or magazine pictures.
3. Fold red and white art paper in half.
4. Glue white paper inside red paper.
5. Follow directions on page 4 for making a standing pop-up card.
6. Glue tree to folded white 6" x 9" (15.0 cm x 22.9 cm) art paper.
7. Match the fold of the tree and the outside of the card before gluing.
   Then glue the tree to the inside of the white paper.
   Be careful not to glue the pop-up section of the card.
8. Write holiday greetings on the inside of the card.

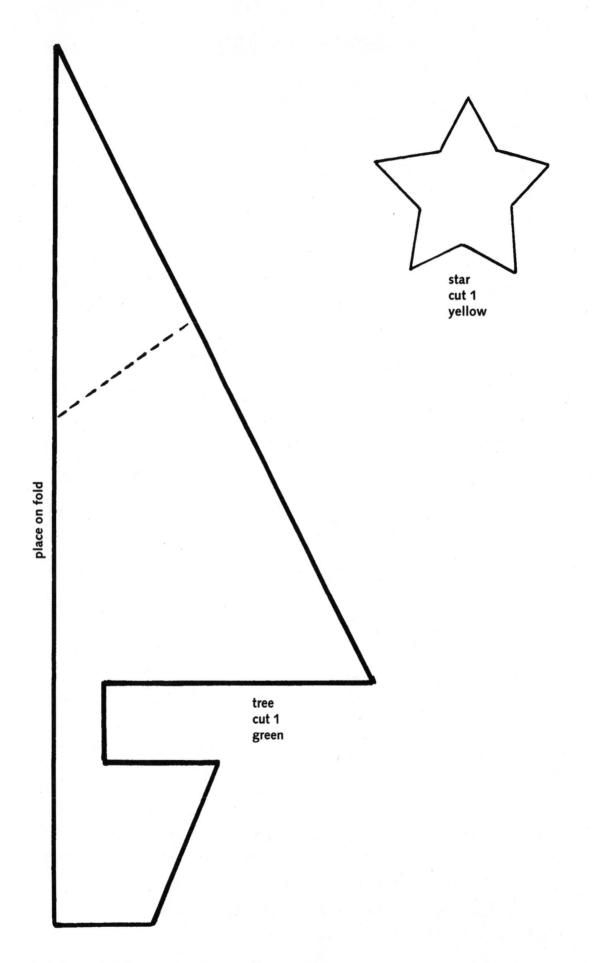

star
cut 1
yellow

tree
cut 1
green

place on fold

26 *Christmas (Holiday Tree)*

Santa Claus

Long ago, a bishop named Nicholas lived in what is now the country of Turkey. He became the patron saint of children. In France, he's *Pere Noel*, in England, he's *Father Christmas*, in Sweden he's *Jultomten*—a small elf who comes in a sleigh pulled by two goats. Dutch settlers in America called him *Sinterklaas*—the American version then became *Santa Claus*. He is the one who comes bearing gifts for all the children of the world.

Materials

Patterns on pages 28–29
Art Paper:
    Red 9" x 12" (22.9 cm x 30.5 cm)
    Green 6" x 9" (15.2 cm x 22.9 cm)
    White 6" x 9" (15.2 cm x 22.9 cm)
    Skin tone 2" x 2" (5.0 cm x 5.0 cm)
Hole punch

Figure A

Procedure

1. Trace and cut out patterns on pages 28–29.
2. Fold red 9" x 12" (22.9 cm x 30.5 cm) art paper in half. Trace Santa's body on the front of the card.
3. Glue Santa's face, beard, mustache, nose, hat trim, belt, buckle, and tassel in place as seen in Figure A.
4. Cut around the Santa shape to the fold. Add details to show the back of Santa on the inside of the card. See Figure B on page 29.
5. Glue green 6" x 9" (15.2 cm x 22.9 cm) art paper to the inside of the card.
6. Write a holiday greeting inside the card.
7. Make snowflakes using white paper and a hole punch. Glue the snowflakes on the inside of the card.

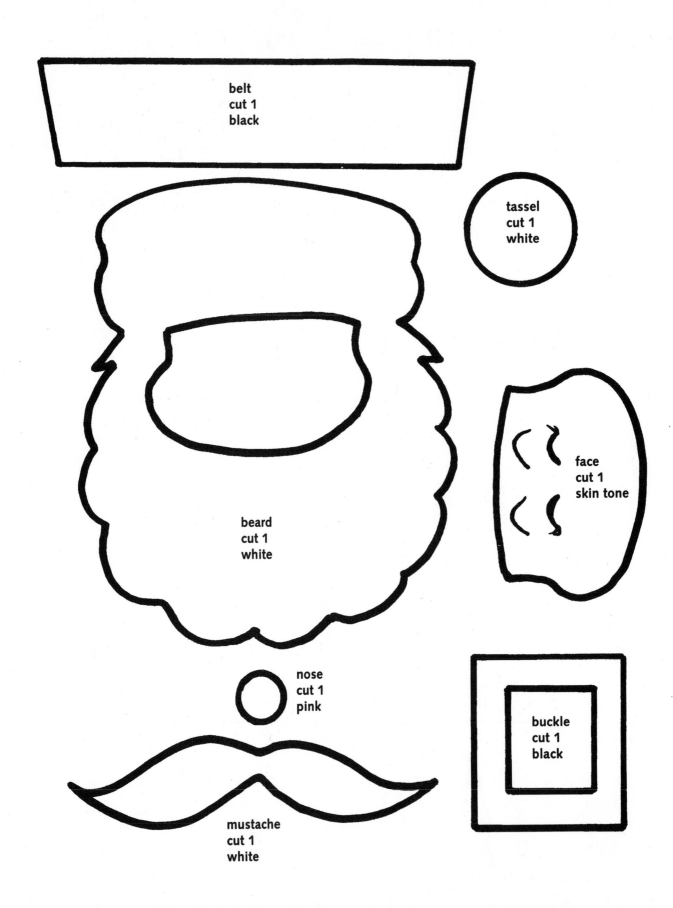

belt
cut 1
black

tassel
cut 1
white

face
cut 1
skin tone

beard
cut 1
white

nose
cut 1
pink

buckle
cut 1
black

mustache
cut 1
white

Greeting Cards for All Occasions ©1995 Fearon Teacher Aids

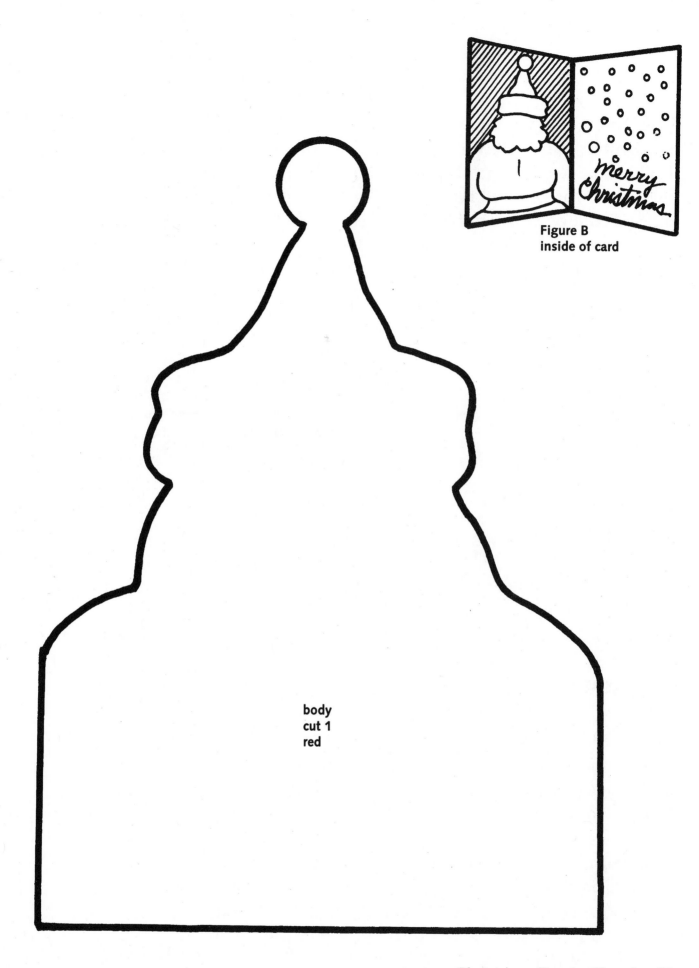

Figure B
inside of card

body
cut 1
red

Feast of Saint Nicholas

The Dutch celebrate a holiday called the Feast of St. Nicholas. While in the United States, St. Nick (or Santa Claus) appears on Christmas Eve, in Holland he appears on December 6th. Children set out wooden shoes filled with carrots and hay for St. Nicholas' great, white horse on the eve of the Feast of St. Nicholas. In return, St. Nicholas will leave sweets and toys in the shoes of all the good children.

Materials

Patterns on pages 31–32
Art Paper:
    Yellow 9" x 12"
        (22.9 cm x 30.5 cm)
    Assorted scraps

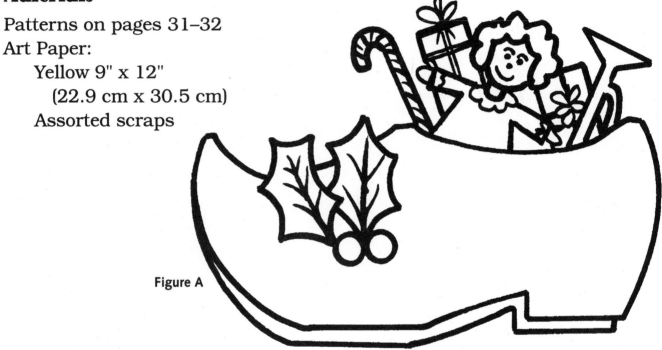

Figure A

Procedure

1. Fold yellow 9" x 12" (22.9 cm x 30.5 cm) art paper in half.
2. Trace wooden shoe pattern on the fold of the yellow art paper. Cut out wooden shoe. Be careful not to cut fold where indicated.
3. Trace and cut out packages, toys, and holly from scraps of art paper.
4. Glue toys and packages to the inside of the wooden shoe, so the cut outs can be seen when the card is open or closed.
5. Decorate packages with crayons or markers.
6. Glue holly leaves to the front of the wooden shoe. Decorate leaves with green marker.
7. Print a holiday message on the inside of the card.

Greeting Cards for All Occasions ©1995 Fearon Teacher Aids

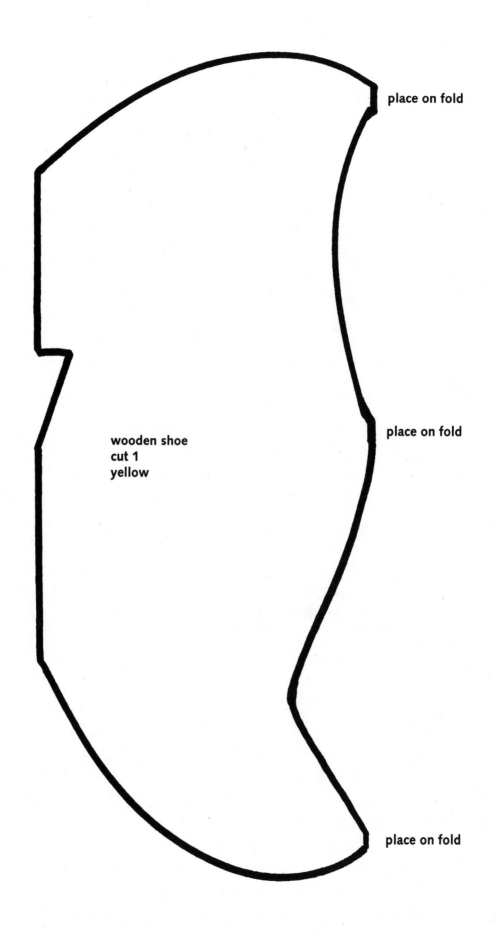

place on fold

place on fold

wooden shoe
cut 1
yellow

place on fold

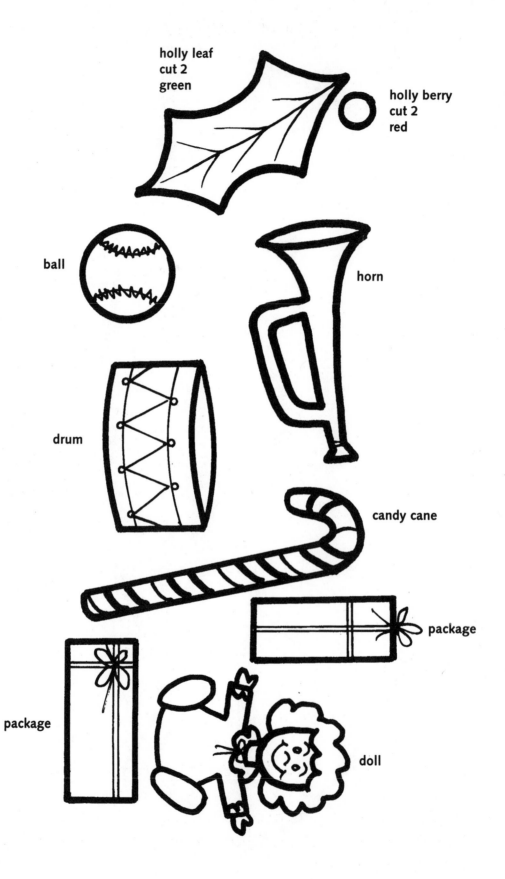

holly leaf
cut 2
green

holly berry
cut 2
red

ball

horn

drum

candy cane

package

package

doll

Greeting Cards for All Occasions ©1995 Fearon Teacher Aids

Stockings

Christmas stockings have been gracing fireplaces for many, many years. Traditionally, a child would hang his or her stocking by the fire so that Santa could fill it with food, toys, and treats. If a child was bad, he or she received only a lump of coal.

Materials

Patterns on page 34
Art Paper:
    Red 9" x 12"
       (22.9 cm x 30.5 cm)
    White 7" x 12"
       (17.7 cm x 30.5 cm)
    Green 3" x 6"
       (7.6 cm x 15.2 cm)
    Assorted scraps
Yarn 6" (15.2 cm)

Procedure

1. Fold white 7" x 12" (17.7 cm x 30.5 cm) art paper in half and then again into fourths.
2. Trace and cut out stocking from folded white paper. Be sure not to cut through the fold where indicated.
3. Trace and cut out holly, berries, candy canes, and gift tag.
4. Glue all cut outs on the stockings. Be careful not to glue cut outs over the folds.
5. Fold red 9" x 12" (22.9 cm x 30.5 cm) art paper in half.
6. Fold stockings accordion style. Glue the first and the fourth stockings to the red paper.
7. Attach the gift tag to the card with yarn.
8. The two center stockings should pop up when the card is opened.

Greeting Cards for All Occasions ©1995 Fearon Teacher Aids

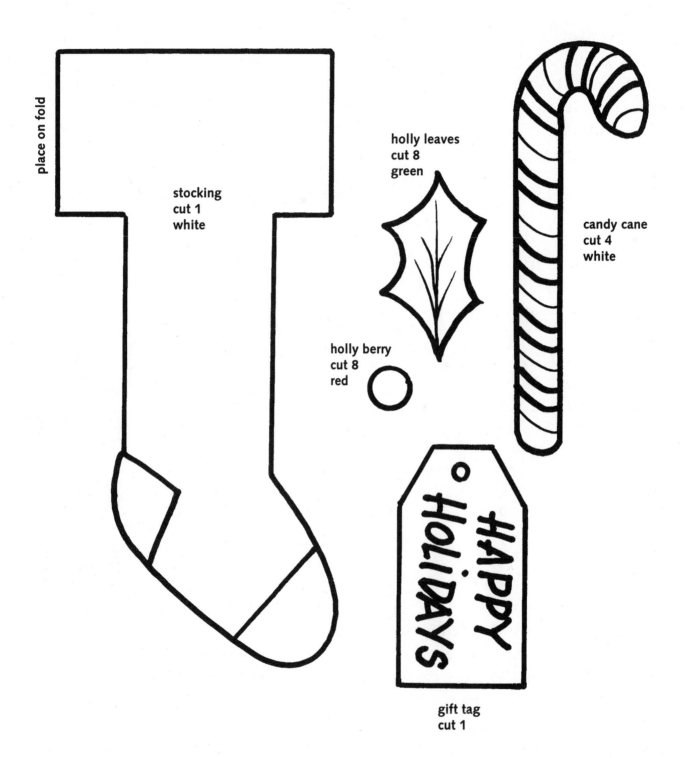

place on fold

stocking
cut 1
white

holly leaves
cut 8
green

holly berry
cut 8
red

candy cane
cut 4
white

HAPPY HOLIDAYS

gift tag
cut 1

Greeting Cards for All Occasions ©1995 Fearon Teacher Aids

Snowman

A common sight in snowy climates is the friendly face of a snowman in the front yard. To make a snowman, you need snow that will stick together, a weather temperature right around freezing, a variety of materials for facial features and accessories, such as carrots, rocks, buttons, hats, scarves, brooms, ear muffs, and so on. Ask students what they would use to make a snowman.

Materials

Pattern on page 36
Art Paper:
> White 9" x 12"
> > (22.9 cm x 30.5 cm)
> Blue 9" x 12"
> > (22.9 cm x 30.5 cm)
> Green 6" x 9"
> > (15.2 cm x 22.9 cm)
Hole punch

Procedure

1. Fold blue 9" x 12" (22.9 cm x 30.5 cm) art paper in half.
2. Trace and cut out the snowman and pine trees.
3. Outline snowman with fine point black felt pen and decorate with crayons or markers. Fold snowman in half with design facing out.
4. Follow directions on page 3 for making a vertical folded pop-up card.
5. Glue snowman to center of pop-up strip matching the folds.
6. Glue 1" x 11" (2.5 cm x 27 cm) white strip along the bottom of the card. Then glue trees on the background.
7. Write holiday greeting on the white strip of paper. Punch holes in the scraps of white paper for snowflakes. Glue snowflakes on the background.

pine tree
cut 3
green

snowman
cut 1
white

Greeting Cards for All Occasions ©1995 Fearon Teacher Aids

Recycled Greeting Cards

Sending greeting cards during the holiday season began in the 1840s in England and only became popular in America in the last hundred years or so. This is primarily due to the increase of postal service. Ask students how many holiday cards they sent this year.

Materials

Art Paper:
    Assorted colors of 9" x 12"
        (22.9 cm x 30.5 cm)
Used greeting cards

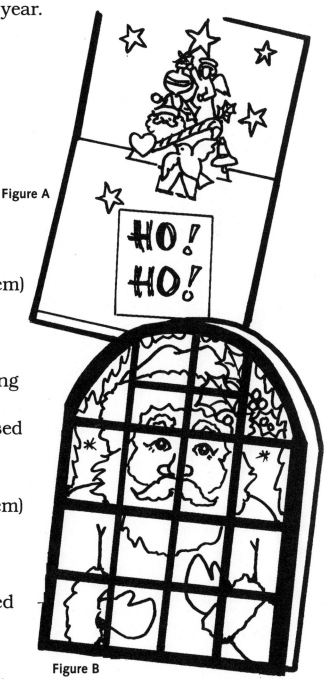

Figure A

Procedure

Figure A
1. Fold green 9" x 12" (22.9 cm x 30.5 cm) art paper in half.
2. Cut out picture from used greeting card.
3. Follow directions on page 2 for making a folded pop-up card.
4. Decorate with other pictures from used greeting cards, crayons, or markers.

Figure B
1. Fold black 9" x 12" (22.9 cm x 30.5 cm) art paper in half.
2. Cut used greeting card in shape of cathedral window or rectangle.
3. Draw lines for cutting on back of used card. Cut out and arrange pieces on folded black art paper. Leave 1/8" (3 mm) between pieces of the picture. Carefully glue in place.
4. Trim black paper around the shape of the picture. Write greeting inside.

Figure B

Make Your Own Envelope

The cards in this book are oversized, therefore it may be difficult to find envelopes to fit them. Also remember that the U.S. Postal Service charges a higher rate to send oversized cards. One solution is to make your own envelopes.

Materials

Art Paper:
    White 12" x 18"
        (30.5 cm x 45.7 cm)

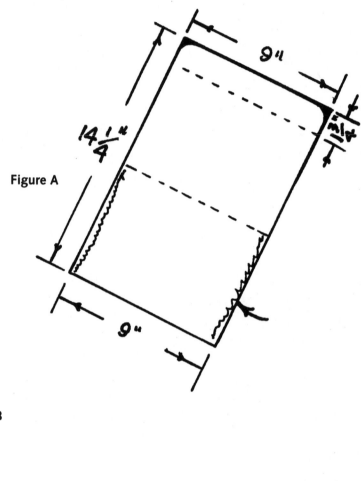

Figure A

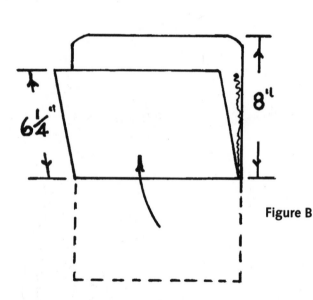

Figure B

Procedure

1. Cut a 9" x 14 1/4" (22.9 cm x 35.6 cm) rectangle from white art paper. See Figure A.
2. Fold up 6 1/4" (15.8 cm) from the bottom to make a flap. Glue the flap along the sides to make a pocket. See Figure B.
3. Fold down 1 3/4" (4.4 cm) from the top. Round the corners of the top flap. See Figure A.
4. Use crayons, markers, or scraps of paper to decorate the outside of the envelope.
5. The same envelope procedure can be used for smaller or larger cards.

Greeting Cards for All Occasions ©1995 Fearon Teacher Aids

Decorate Your Envelope

After making a fun holiday greeting card, send some extra cheer by decorating the outside of the envelope, too. This can be done whether you've made your own envelopes or used standard ones.

Materials

Art Paper:
    White, red, or
    green scraps

Figure A

Figure B

Procedure

Figure A
1. Draw red lines across the envelope to look like ribbon.
2. Trace and cut out bow from red art paper. Glue bow to the front of the envelope.
3. Trace and cut out address card from white art paper.
4. Glue address card to front of envelope.

Figure B
1. Draw red lines across corners of the envelope to look like ribbon.
2. Trace and cut out holly leaves and berries.
3. Trace and cut out address card from white art paper.
4. Glue address card to front of envelope.

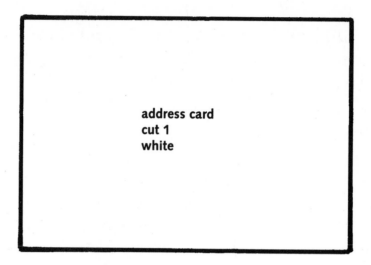

address card
cut 1
white

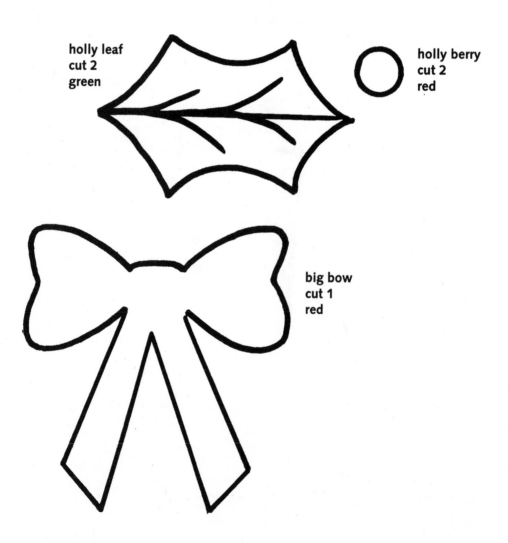

holly leaf
cut 2
green

holly berry
cut 2
red

big bow
cut 1
red

Greeting Cards for All Occasions ©1995 Fearon Teacher Aids

Kwanzaa

Kwanzaa means *first* in the Swahili language of Africa and is a celebration of the first harvest. In the United States, African Americans celebrate their African heritage. Traditional Kwanzaa celebrations include fruits and vegetables (for unity), a straw mat (for tradition), an ear of corn representing each child, a drinking cup, and a *kinara* (a 7-branched candle holder symbolizing the continent and people of Africa). The seven candles in the kinara represent seven life principles: unity, self-determination, work and responsibility, cooperation, purpose, creativity, and faith. The center candle is black for the dark skin of African people, three candles are green for the green hills of Africa, three candles are red for the blood that African Americans have shed for freedom. Each night, a candle is lit and small homemade gifts are exchanged, such as clothes, toys, and beads. On the last day, family and friends share a feast called the *karamu* that includes music and dancing.

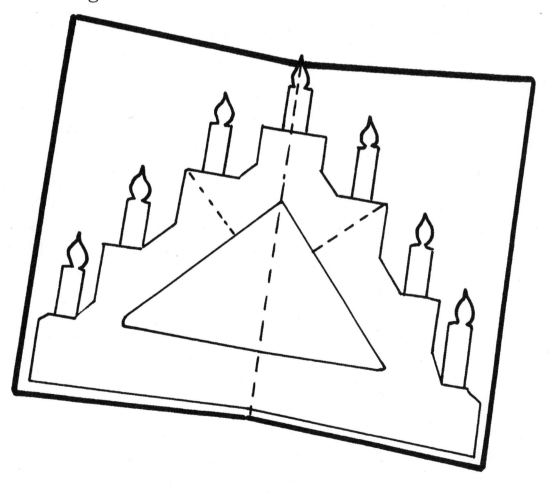

Materials

Patterns on page 43
Art Paper:
    Brown 9" x 12" (22.9 cm x 30.5 cm)
    Black 9" x 12" (22.9 cm x 30.5 cm)
    Red 4" x 4" (10.2 cm x 10.2 cm)
    Green 4" x 4" (10.2 cm x 10.2 cm)
    Orange scraps

Procedure

1. Fold the black 9" x 12" (22.9 cm x 30.5 cm) art paper in half and place the candle holder on the fold. Trace and cut out the candle holder.
2. Trace and cut out one black candle, three red candles, and three green candles.
3. Cut out seven orange flames from candle pattern. Glue the candles and flames together.
4. Follow directions on page 4 for making a standing pop-up card.
5. Glue three green candles on the left, three red candles on the right, and the black candle in the center.
6. Fold brown 9" x 12" (22.9 cm x 30.5 cm) paper in half. Glue the bottom four candles of the candle holder to the inside of the card. Do not glue top three candles to the brown paper.
7. When the card is opened the top three candles should pop up.
8. Write greeting inside card.

Greeting Cards for All Occasions ©1995 Fearon Teacher Aids

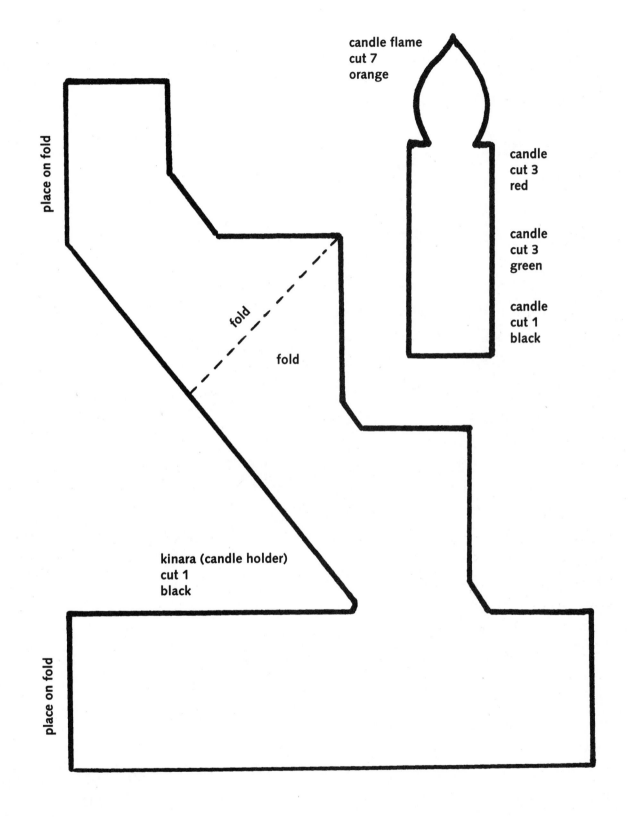

candle flame
cut 7
orange

candle
cut 3
red

candle
cut 3
green

candle
cut 1
black

place on fold

fold

fold

kinara (candle holder)
cut 1
black

place on fold

New Year's Day

Happy New Year! In the United States, New Year's Day is a happy celebration of looking forward to a new and exciting year. It's also a time to make resolutions for change. A *resolution* is a decision to make something better. Is there something you would like to do better in the new year? Ask students to try and think of three New Year's resolutions to write inside of their cards.

Materials

Pattern on page 45
Art Paper:
    Skin tone 9" x 12"
       (22.9 cm x 30.5 cm)
    Purple 9" x 12"
       (22.9 cm x 30.5 cm)
    Assorted scraps

Procedure

1. Reproduce the pattern on page 45 on skin tone art paper.
2. Fold both the skin tone and purple art paper in half.
3. Outline the design on the skin tone paper with a black felt pen.
4. Decorate the baby with crayons.
5. Carefully cut along the solid line from the edge of the paper, around the baby, to the other edge of the paper.
6. Follow directions on page 4 for making a standing pop-up card.
7. Match the folds for the baby and the outside of the card before gluing. Then glue the design to the inside of the purple paper. Be careful not to glue the pop-up section of the card.
8. Use crayons and scrap paper to decorate the background of the card.

Greeting Cards for All Occasions ©1995 Fearon Teacher Aids

The New Year

Martin Luther King, Jr. Birthday

This day celebrates the birthday of famous civil rights leader, Martin Luther King, Jr. In his famous speech "I Have a Dream," one of the dreams he spoke about was that his "four little children will one day live in a nation where they will not be judged by the color of their skin but by the content of their character." He devoted his life to trying to make this dream come true. Ask students what they think Dr. King meant by this statement.

Materials

Patterns on page 47
Art Paper
 Light brown 4 1/2" x 11"
  (11.4 cm x 27 cm)
 Yellow 9" x 12"
  (22.9 cm x 30.5 cm)
 Black 4" x 6"
  (10.2 cm x 15.2 cm)
 Assorted scraps

Procedure

1. Trace and cut Figure 1 from black 4" x 6" (10.2 cm x 15.2 cm) art paper.
2. Trace and cut out three of Figure 2 and three of Figure 3 from dark brown, black, and pink art paper.
3. Fold the light brown and yellow art papers in half.
4. Fold Figure 1 in half.
5. Follow the directions on page 4 for making a standing pop-up card.
6. Match the fold of Figure 1 to the fold of the light brown paper. Then glue Figure 1 one inch (2.5 cm) from the bottom of the light brown paper.
7. Match the folds for the inside and outside of the card before gluing. Be careful not to glue the pop-up section of the card.
8. Glue multicolored cut outs of Figures 2 and 3 to the bottom of the light brown paper to look like a crowd of people.
9. Cut out the rectangle with the message. Trace over message with a black felt pen and glue to the yellow background.

Greeting Cards for All Occasions ©1995 Fearon Teacher Aids

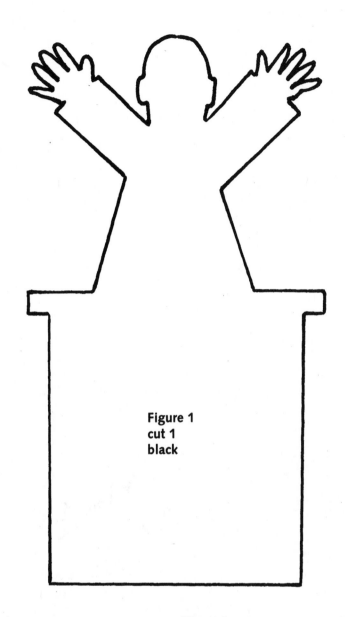

Figure 1
cut 1
black

Figure 3
cut 3 of each color
dark brown
black
pink

Figure 2
cut 3 of each color
dark brown
black
pink

message
cut 1
white

HE HAD A
DREAM !

Flip-Top Snowperson

There's nothing more fun to do after a big snowfall than make a snowperson. If the conditions are right and the snow sticks together, you can make a whole family of snow people in your front yard. A snowperson can be dressed to look like just about anyone. Ask students how they would dress their snowpersons.

Materials

Patterns on page 49
Art Paper:
    White 9" x 12"
      (22.9 cm x 30.5 cm)
    Black 6" x 9"
      (15.2 cm x 22.9 cm)
    Red 6" x 9"
      (15.2 cm x 22.9 cm)
    Blue, orange, and
    green scraps

Procedure

1. Fold white 9" x 12" (22.9 cm x 30.5 cm) art paper
   in half, vertically. Then fold 3 1/2" (8.9 cm) down from the top.
2. Trace and cut out all of the pattern pieces.
3. Draw a circle for the snowperson's head in the center of the
   4 1/2" x 12" (11.4 cm x 30.5 cm) white art paper.
4. Glue nose, scarf, and ear muffs on the snowperson.
   Add other details with crayons or markers.
5. Glue hat and hat band to the top of the 3 1/2" (8.9 cm) white
   flap. When the flap is down the hat should appear on the
   snowperson's head.
6. Write greeting or cheerful note under the flap.

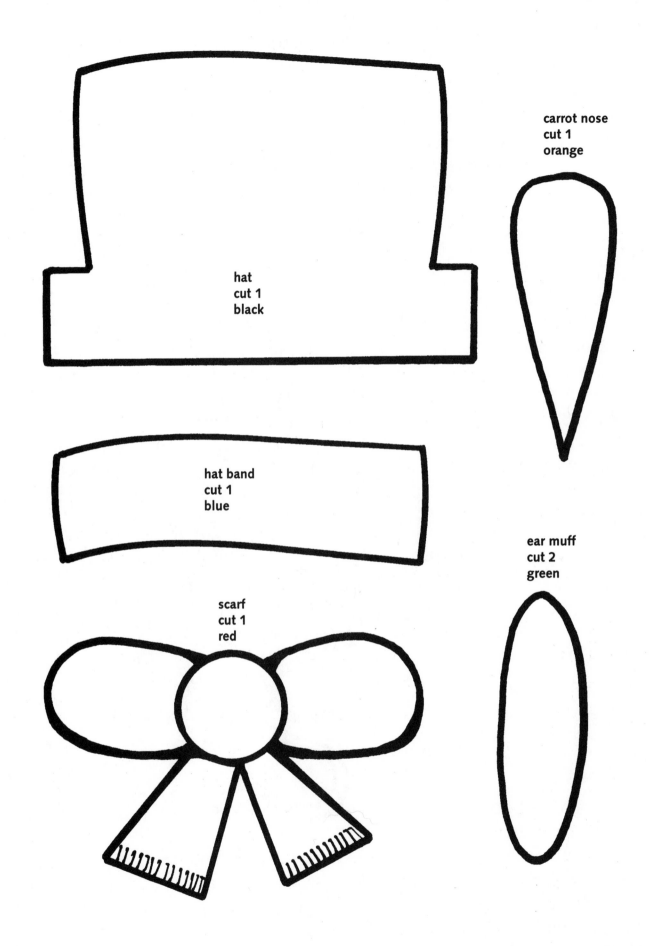

carrot nose
cut 1
orange

hat
cut 1
black

hat band
cut 1
blue

ear muff
cut 2
green

scarf
cut 1
red

Mittens

Mittens are wonderful for keeping hands warm in the winter. They are warmer than gloves because all your fingers stay close together. Gloves on the other hand, keep your fingers apart which creates less heat. Ask students what other clothes they wear only in the winter.

Materials

Patterns on page 51
Art Paper:
    Red 6 1/2" x 9"
      (16.5 cm x 22.9 cm)
    White 4" x 4"
      (10. 2 cm x 10.2 cm)
    Green 3" x 4"
      (7.6 cm x 10.2 cm)
Hole punch
Green yarn 12" (30.5 cm)

Procedure

1. Trace and cut out mittens, trees, and mitten cuffs.
2. Glue cuffs and trees to mittens.
3. Punch holes in each mitten cuff. Use yarn to tie mittens together.
4. Write greeting on mitten cuffs.

Greeting Cards for All Occasions ©1995 Fearon Teacher Aids

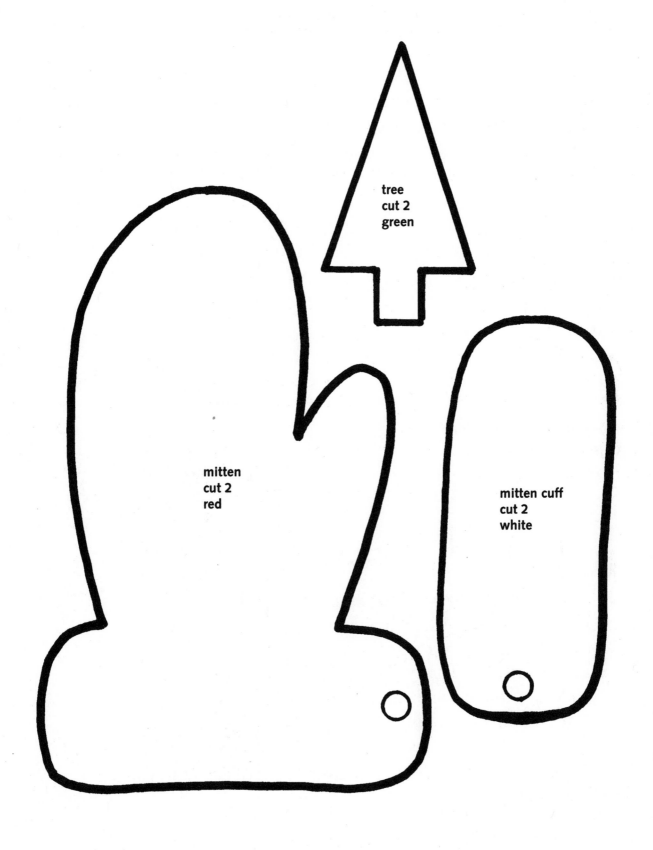

tree
cut 2
green

mitten
cut 2
red

mitten cuff
cut 2
white

Chinese New Year

In China, the dragon is a symbol of goodness and strength. The Chinese use the dragon during their New Year's celebration to lead the Festival of Lanterns parade. People gather together with lighted lanterns and form a parade in the street. Leading the way is a huge dragon. It is constructed of bamboo that is covered with paper or silk. Sometimes this dragon is up to 100 feet (30.48 m) long, requiring 50 men and boys to carry it on their shoulders. Only their feet show as they start winding their way through the streets.

Materials

Pattern on page 53
Art Paper:
    Pink 9" x 12"
        (22.9 cm x 30.5 cm)
    White 9" x 12"
        (22.9 cm x 30.5 cm)

Procedure

1. Reproduce dragon on white 9" x 12" (22.9 cm x 30.5 cm) art paper. Decorate with crayons or markers.
2. Fold the white and pink art papers in half.
3. Measure 5" (12.7 cm) from the bottom of the white art paper. Lightly draw a pencil line from the edge of the paper to the design. Do not draw on the dragon.
4. Carefully cut along the pencil line up to the design. Then cut around the dragon and continue cutting along the pencil line to the edge of the paper.
5. Follow directions on page 4 for making a standing pop-up card.
6. Match the folds for the inside and outside of the card before gluing. Then glue the design to the inside of the pink paper. Be careful not to glue the pop-up section of the card.
7. Write greetings on the inside of the card, if desired.

Greeting Cards for All Occasions ©1995 Fearon Teacher Aids

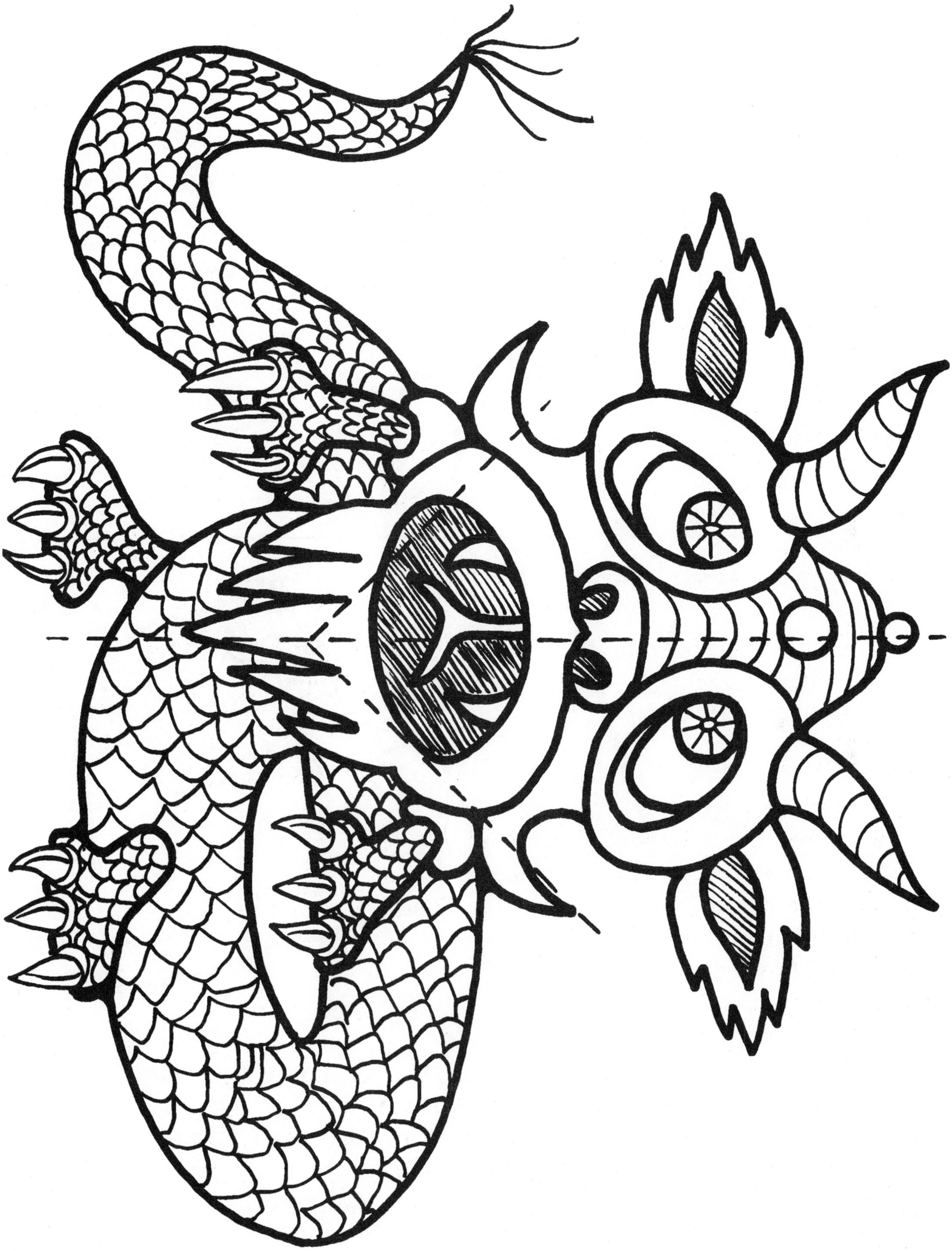

Valentine Bee

Who was St. Valentine? One legend claims that St. Valentine, a priest in Rome, was thrown in jail and fell in love with the jailer's daughter. He wrote her a letter signed, "From your Valentine." This was said to be the first valentine. Today, valentines include symbols of love, such as hearts, flowers, doves, and cupids. Ask students if they can think of someone they would like to give a valentine to.

Materials

Patterns on page 55
Art Paper:
> Pink 9" x 12"
>> (22.9 cm x 30.5 cm)
> Yellow 4" x 8"
>> (10.2 cm x 20.3 cm)
> Red 4" x 6"
>> (10.2 cm x 15.2 cm)
> Green 3" x 6"
>> (7.6 cm x 15.2 cm)

Procedure

1. Fold pink 9" x 12" (22.9 cm x 30.5 cm) art paper in half.
2. Trace and cut out patterns on page 55.
3. Outline the pattern pieces with a black felt pen. Decorate the pieces with crayons or markers.
4. Follow directions on page 2 for making a folded pop-up card.
5. Glue the bee cut out to the pop-up section.
6. Arrange and glue the cut outs on the inside of the card.
7. Print a valentine message on one of the large hearts with a felt pen.

Greeting Cards for All Occasions ©1995 Fearon Teacher Aids

leaf
cut 2
green

grass
cut 1
green

bee
cut 1
yellow

stem
cut 1
green

large heart
cut 2
red

small heart
cut 2
red

medium heart
cut 2
red

Valentine Dog

Valentine's Day is not just for sweethearts but for friends, too. Tell a friend or family member how much you like him or her with a special handmade valentine. Make someone's day by sending a valentine.

Materials

Patterns on page 57
Art Paper:
    White 6" x 9" (15.2 cm x 22.9 cm)
    Red 6" x 12" (15.2 cm x 30.5 cm)

Procedure

1. Fold red 6" x 12" (15.2 cm x 30.5 cm) art paper in half.
2. Trace and cut out patterns on page 57.
3. Outline the pattern pieces with a black felt pen.
   Decorate the pieces with crayons.
4. Follow directions on page 2 for making a folded pop-up card.
5. Glue dog cut out to the pop-up section.
6. Arrange and glue the cut outs on the inside of the card.
7. Print a valentine message on the large hearts with a black felt pen.

Greeting Cards for All Occasions ©1995 Fearon Teacher Aids

large heart
cut 1
white

medium heart
cut 2
white

small heart
cut 2
white

dog
cut 1
white

Valentine's Frog

Ask students if they have ever received a valentine from a frog. Valentines don't need to be mushy or sweet. Encourage each student to send a friend a funny valentine.

Materials

Patterns on page 59
Art Paper:
    Red 9" x 12"
      (22.9 cm x 30.5 cm)
    Green 6" x 9"
      (15.2 cm x 22.9 cm)
    Pink 6" x 9"
      (15.2 cm x 22.9 cm)

Figure A
inside

Figure B
cover

Procedure

1. Measure and fold 3" (7.6 cm) on each side of the red 9" x 12" (22.9 cm x 30.5 cm) art paper. See Figure A.
2. Trace and cut out hearts and frog.
3. Outline the frog with a black felt pen.
4. Glue frog and hearts to the inside of the card.
5. Fold over the two 3" (7.6 cm) flaps on the front of the card. Glue half of the large heart to the right side of the cover.
6. Glue half of one of the medium hearts to the left side of the cover.
7. Print valentine message on the hearts.

Greeting Cards for All Occasions ©1995 Fearon Teacher Aids

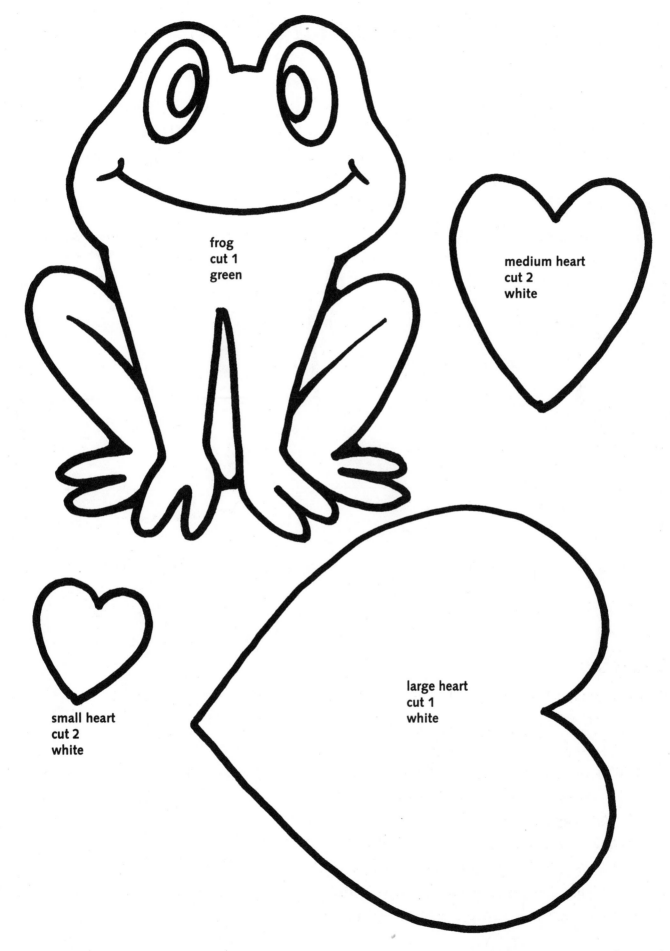

frog
cut 1
green

medium heart
cut 2
white

small heart
cut 2
white

large heart
cut 1
white

Washington

George Washington was the first president of the United States and became known as the "Father of Our Country." One of the most colorful myths regarding Washington was his chopping down a cherry tree as a young boy. When his father confronted him, Washington immediately confessed, stating, "I cannot tell a lie." This myth helped promote Washington as a truthful person.

Materials

Pattern on page 61
Art Paper:
  Red 9" x 12" (22.9 cm x 30.5 cm)
  Black 6" x 9" (15.2 cm x 22.9 cm)
  White 9" x 12" (22.9 cm x 30.5 cm)
  Blue 2" x 2" (5.0 cm x 5.0 cm)

Figure A

Procedure

1. Fold red 9" x 12" (22.9 cm x 30.5 cm) art paper in half.
2. Trace and cut out pattern on black art paper.
3. Glue pattern to front of folded red art paper.
4. Cut two 1/2" x 4" (1.3 cm x 10.2 cm) strips of white paper.
5. Cut one 1 1/2" x 1 3/4" (3.9 cm x 4.4 cm) rectangle from blue art paper.
6. Trace and cut out one star from white art paper.
7. Glue cut outs below the silhouette of Washington on the cover of the card. See Figure A.
8. Write message or poem on white 5" x 8" (12.7 cm x 20.3 cm) rectangle. Glue to inside of card.

Greeting Cards for All Occasions ©1995 Fearon Teacher Aids

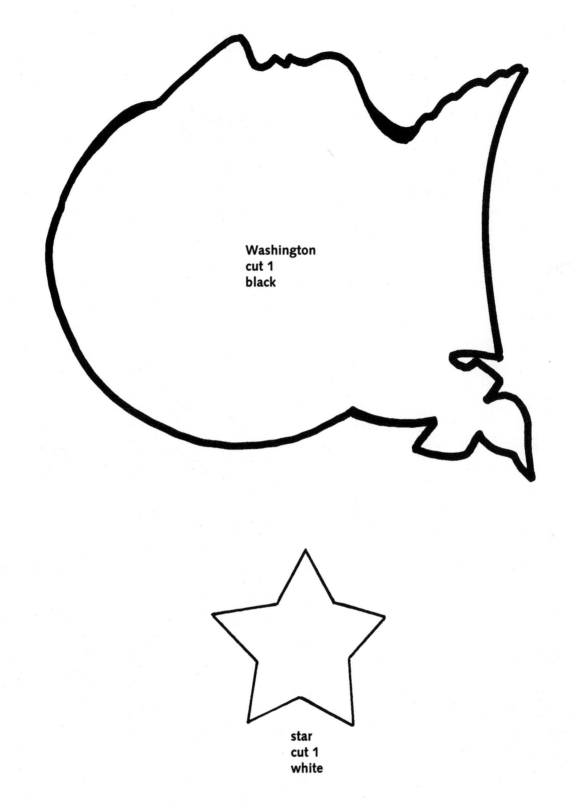

Washington
cut 1
black

star
cut 1
white

Lincoln

Abraham Lincoln was the 16th president of the United States. His life became the true American Dream. Born in a log cabin to a poor family, he was not able to go to school. Lincoln had to educate himself. He read from the Bible, Shakespeare, and whatever law books he could find. This hard work and dedication is what helped him become president.

Materials

Pattern on page 63
Art Paper:
    Red 9" x 12" (22.9 cm x 30.5 cm)
    Black 6" x 9" (15.2 cm x 22.9 cm)
    White 9" x 12" (22.9 cm x 30.5 cm)
    Blue 2" x 2" (5.0 cm x 5.0 cm)

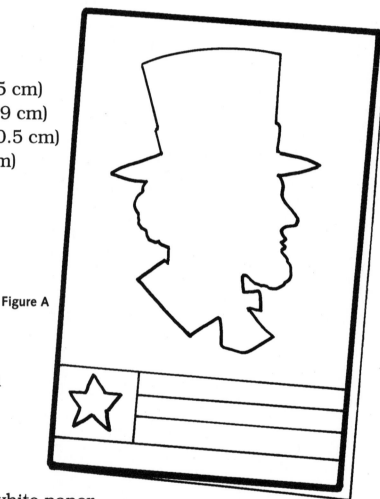

Figure A

Procedure

1. Fold red 9" x 12" (22.9 cm x 30.5 cm) art paper in half.
2. Trace and cut out pattern on black art paper.
3. Glue pattern to front of folded red art paper.
4. Cut two 1/2" x 4" (1.3 cm x 10.2 cm) strips of white paper.
5. Cut one 1 1/2" x 1 3/4" (3.9 cm x 4.4 cm) rectangle from blue art paper.
6. Trace and cut out one star from white art paper.
7. Glue cut outs below the silhouette of Lincoln on the cover of the card. See Figure A.
8. Write or print message or poem on white 5" x 8" (12.7 cm x 20.3 cm) rectangle. Glue to the inside of the card.

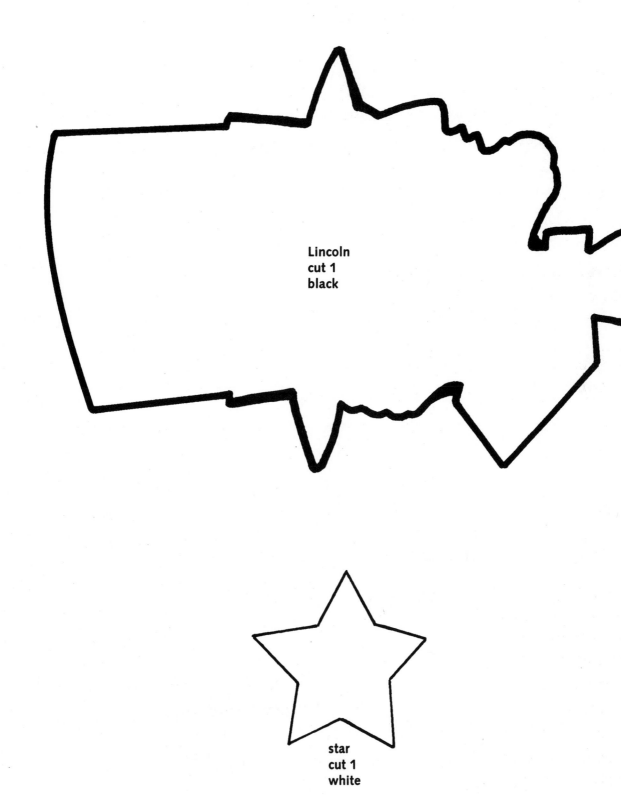

Lincoln
cut 1
black

star
cut 1
white

Shamrock

The shamrock is a green, three-leafed plant. It is also the national plant of Ireland where St. Patrick's Day originates. St. Patrick was a priest around whom many legends were formed.

Materials

Pattern on page 65
Art Paper:
    Green 9" x 12" (22.9 cm x 30.5 cm)
    Pink scrap

Procedure

1. Fold green 9" x 12" (22.9 cm x 30.5 cm) art paper in half.
2. Trace and cut out shamrock on green art paper. Do not cut through the fold.
3. Trace and cut out heart. Glue heart on front of shamrock.
4. Write St. Patrick's Day greeting inside card.

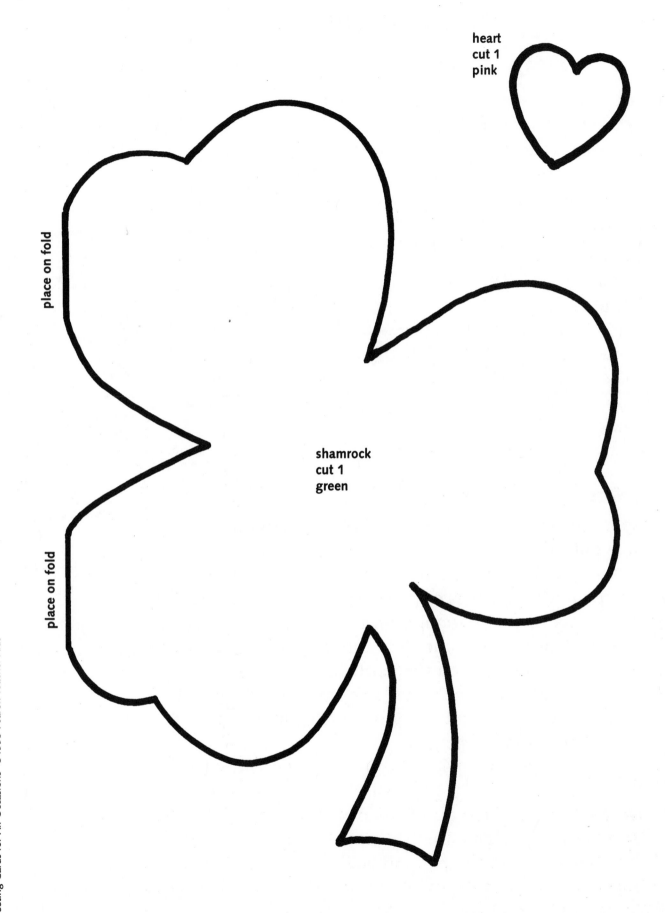

heart
cut 1
pink

place on fold

place on fold

shamrock
cut 1
green

Leprechaun

The leprechaun's origin is in Irish legend. He is a mischievous fairy in the form of a little old man. Legend tells us the leprechaun can reveal a buried crock of gold to anyone who manages to catch him. Encourage students to think of clever ways to catch a leprechaun.

Materials

Pattern on page 67
Art Paper:
    Light green 9" x 12"
      (22.9 cm x 30.5 cm)
    White 9" x 12"
      (22.9 cm x 30.5 cm)
    Yellow scrap
    Black scrap

Procedure

1. Reproduce the pattern on page 67 on white art paper.
2. Fold both the light green and white art papers in half.
3. Outline the leprechaun design with a black felt pen.
4. Decorate with crayons or markers.
5. Measure 4 3/4" (12.1 cm) from the bottom of the light green paper. Lightly draw a pencil line from the edge of the paper to the design. Do not draw the line on the leprechaun.
6. Carefully cut along the pencil line up to the design. Then cut around the design and continue cutting along the pencil line to the edge of the paper.
7. Follow directions on page 4 for making a standing pop-up card.
8. Match the folds for the inside and outside of the card before gluing. Then glue the design to the inside of the light green paper. Be careful not to glue the pop-up section of the card.
9. Trace and cut out the pot and gold. Glue to the bottom of the card.
10. Use crayons and scrap paper to decorate the background of the card.
11. Write a St. Patrick's Day greeting on the inside of the card.

Greeting Cards for All Occasions ©1995 Fearon Teacher Aids

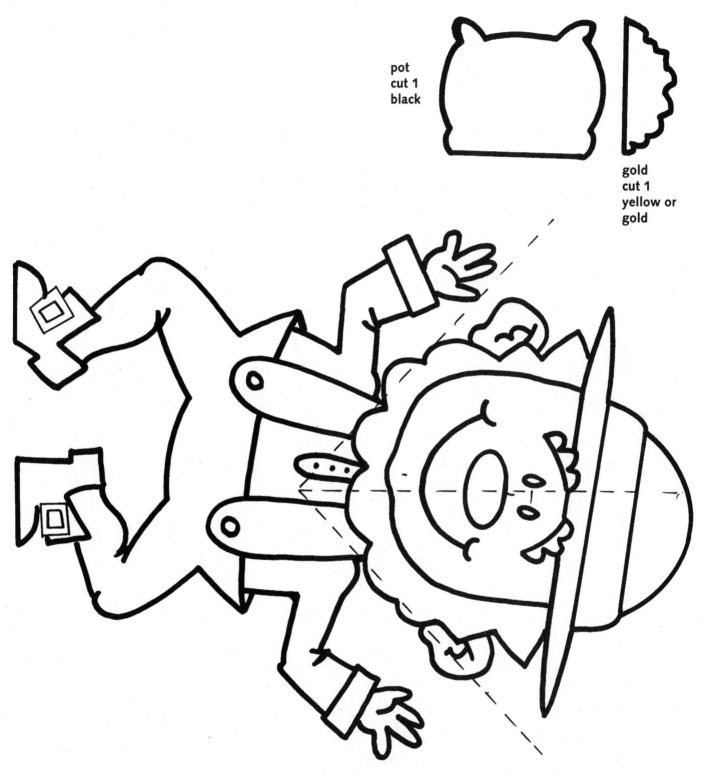

pot
cut 1
black

gold
cut 1
yellow or
gold

Eid

Watching from the top of a mosque, holy men of the Muslim faith watch eagerly for the new moon. When the beautiful crescent moon glows in the sky, the celebration begins. Eid, which comes twice a year, celebrates faith, devotion, and discipline. The second celebration is preceded with a 30-day fast called *Ramadan*. Again, the new crescent moon will announce the coming of Eid. Muslims celebrate by giving gifts to children and donating to charities.

Materials

Patterns on page 69
Art Paper:
    Purple 9" x 12" (22.9 cm x 30.5 cm)
    Blue 1" x 3" (2.5 cm x 7.6 cm)
    Red 1 1/2" x 3" (3.9 cm x 7.6 cm)
    Green 2" x 5" (5.0 cm x 12.7 cm)
    Assorted scraps
    Gold or silver (optional)
Gold or silver art pen (optional)

Procedure

1. Fold purple 9" x 12" (22.9 cm x 30.5 cm) art paper in half.
2. Trace and cut out the various sizes of domes from different colors of art paper.
3. Arrange red, blue, and green strips on the front of the purple art paper. Glue strips in place and add domes on top of each building.
4. Use scrap paper for other buildings on the front of the card.
5. Trace and cut out moon and star from gold or silver paper.
6. Glue the moon and star above the buildings.
7. Use scraps to make doors and windows. Add details to the domes with gold or silver art pens.
8. Write message inside the card.

Greeting Cards for All Occasions ©1995 Fearon Teacher Aids

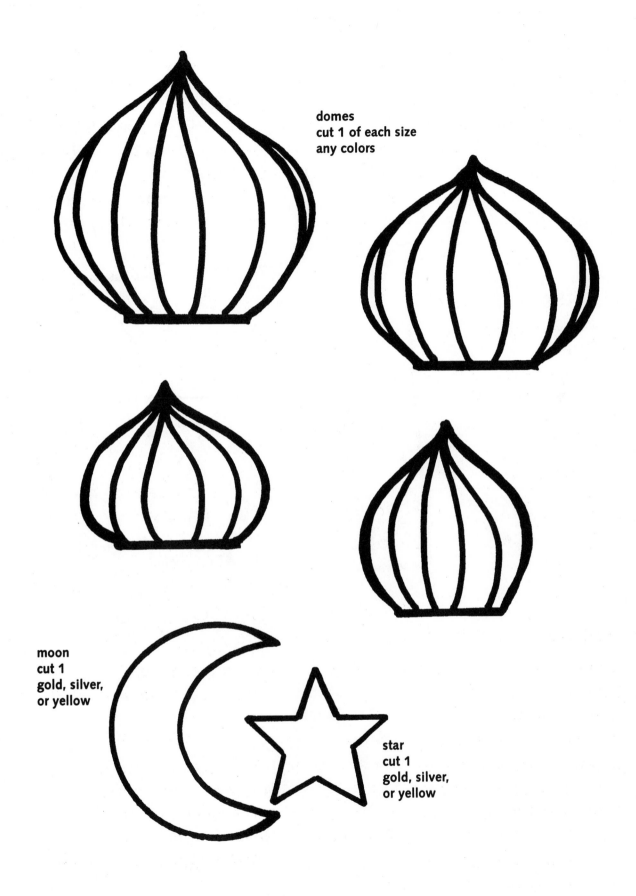

domes
cut 1 of each size
any colors

moon
cut 1
gold, silver,
or yellow

star
cut 1
gold, silver,
or yellow

Easter Eggs

Egg dying has a long history. In ancient spring festivals of Egypt, Persia, Greece, and Rome, eggs were dyed and eaten. Today in many countries, eggs are part of Easter games and festivities. Sometimes people hide eggs and have Easter egg hunts in their homes or backyards.

Materials

Pattern on page 71
Art Paper:
    Yellow 9" x 12"
      (22.9 cm x 30.5 cm)
    White 8 1/2" x 11"
      (21 cm x 27 cm)
    Assorted scraps

Procedure

1. Fold yellow 9" x 12" (22.9 cm x 30.5 cm) art paper in half.
2. Reproduce pattern on page 71 on white art paper.
3. Decorate with crayons or markers.
4. Carefully cut along the solid line from the edge of the paper, around the bunny, to the other edge of the paper.
5. Follow directions on page 4 for making a standing pop-up card.
6. Match the folds for the inside and outside of the card before gluing. Then glue the bunny to the inside of the yellow paper. Be careful not to glue the pop-up section of the card.
7. Use crayons and scrap paper to decorate the background of the card.

Greeting Cards for All Occasions ©1995 Fearon Teacher Aids

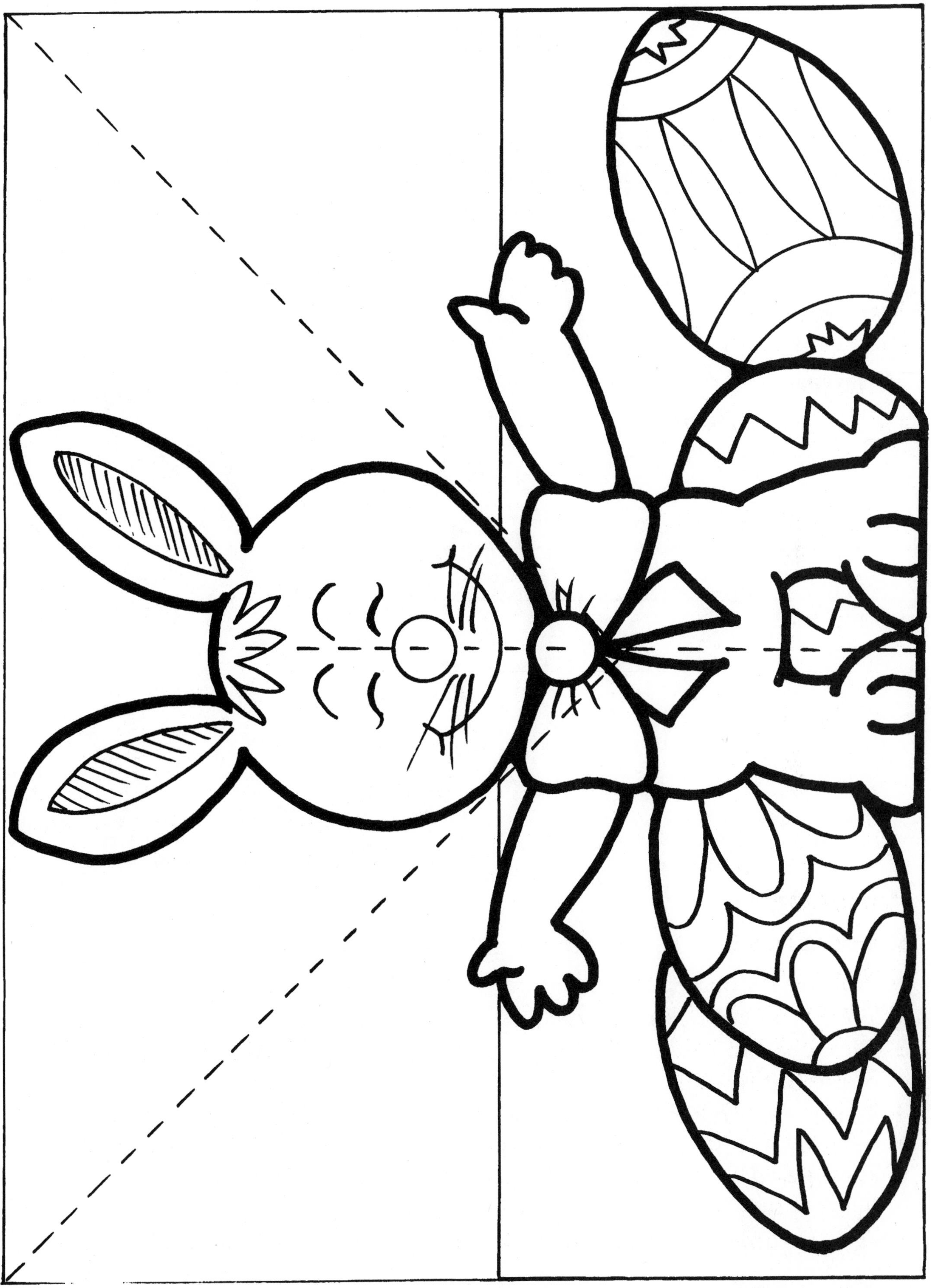

Circle Bunny

Since ancient times, the rabbit has been a symbol of the moon. And since the timing of Easter depends on the phase of the moon, the rabbit has become a symbol associated with Easter. The Easter bunny custom came to us from Germany. German children would build large nests outside or in barns for the Easter bunny to lay eggs in on Easter Eve. Today, these nests appear inside Easter baskets.

Materials

Patterns on page 73
Art Paper:
    2 Yellow 9" x 12"
      (22.9 cm x 30.5 cm)
    Pink scraps
    White scraps
Cotton balls

Figure A

Procedure

1. Fold yellow 9" x 12" (22.9 cm x 30.5 cm) art paper in half.
2. Trace and cut out patterns on page 73.
3. Glue head to the front of the body. The fold should be at the top of the bunny.
4. Trace and cut out nose from pink art paper. Glue nose and eyes to head. Then decorate with crayons. See Figure A.
5. Glue two feet to front of card and two feet to back of card.
6. Print greeting inside of card.
7. Glue cotton ball to back of card for tail.

Greeting Cards for All Occasions ©1995 Fearon Teacher Aids

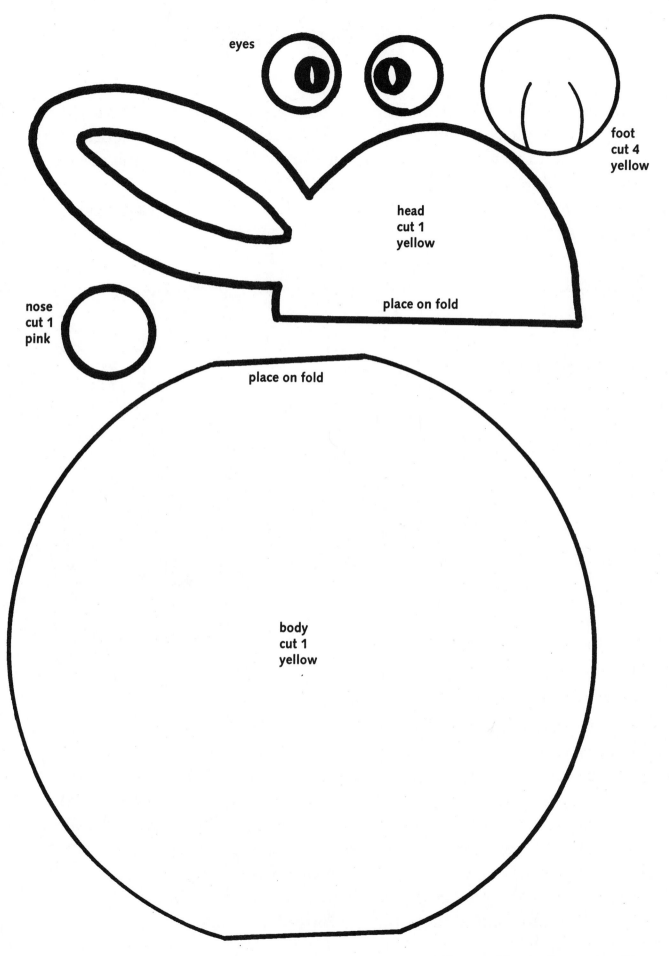

eyes

foot
cut 4
yellow

head
cut 1
yellow

place on fold

nose
cut 1
pink

place on fold

body
cut 1
yellow

Spring Chick

Easter probably got its name from *Eostre*, an ancient spring goddess. Though Easter is the most important Christian holiday celebrated throughout the world, many also celebrate Easter as a time of life renewing itself—the coming of spring.

Materials

Pattern on page 75
Art Paper:
    Yellow 9" x 12"
       (22.9 cm x 30.5 cm)
    White 8 1/2" x 11"
       (21 cm x 27 cm)
    Assorted scraps

Procedure

1. Fold yellow 9" x 12" (22.9 cm x 30.5 cm) art paper in half.
2. Reproduce pattern on page 75 on white paper.
3. Decorate pattern with crayons or markers.
4. Carefully cut along the solid line from the edge of the paper, around the chick, to the other edge of the paper.
5. Follow directions on page 4 for making a standing pop-up card.
6. Match the folds for the inside and outside of the card before gluing. Then glue the chick to the inside of the yellow paper. Be careful not to glue the pop-up section of the card.
7. Use crayons and scrap paper to decorate the background of the card.
8. Write a spring greeting on the inside of the card.

Greeting Cards for All Occasions ©1995 Fearon Teacher Aids

Earth Day

This day reminds us of how we can keep our world clean and healthy. There are a lot of ways we can help. We can pick up trash from our neighborhood or schoolyard. We can save trees by recycling newspaper. We can recycle glass and plastic and keep our rivers and oceans free of litter. Ask students to think of ways to celebrate Earth Day every day.

Materials

Patterns on page 77
Art Paper:
    Blue 9" x 12"
      (22.9 cm x 30.5 cm)
    Light blue 4" x 4"
      (7.6 cm x 7.6 cm)
    Green 1 1/2" x 5 1/2"
      (3.9 cm x 14 cm)
    Assorted scraps
    Pink, light brown,
      dark brown, yellow
Cardboard 1" x 1"
  (2.5 cm x 2.5 cm)

Figure A

Procedure

1. Fold blue 9" x 12" (22.9 cm x 30.5 cm) art paper in half.
2. Trace and cut out patterns on page 77. Draw land on the globe.
3. Write Earth Day message on green 1 1/2" x 5" (3.9 cm x 14 cm) art paper.
4. Glue 1" x 1" (2.5 cm x 2.5 cm) cardboard square behind globe for a 3-dimensional effect. Then glue the globe to the front of the card.
5. Glue the multicolored arms under the globe. See Figure A.
6. Glue green banner on the front of the card overlapping the bottom of the arms.
7. Use crayons to add stars to the background. If desired, add a toothpick flag representing your country.

Greeting Cards for All Occasions ©1995 Fearon Teacher Aids

globe
cut 1
light blue

arm
cut 1 of each color
pink
light brown
dark brown
yellow
black

banner
cut 1
green

EARTH DAY
WE ALL NEED TO HELP

May Day

May Day is a celebration of the coming of spring and nature's renewal. In Europe, people used to celebrate May Day by selecting the fairest village maiden as Queen of the May and dancing around the maypole. A maypole is a tall rail with spring flowers adorning the top. Streamers, representing the sun's rays, flow down around it. Dancers hold onto these streamers as they revolve around the maypole.

Materials

Patterns on page 79
Art Paper:
    Purple 9" x 12"
      (22.9 cm x 30.5 cm)
    Light blue 9" x 12"
      (22.9 cm x 30.5 cm)
    Assorted scraps

Procedure

1. Fold both the light blue and purple art paper in half.
2. Draw a maypole with multicolored streamers on the center fold of the light blue paper.
3. Measure 4 3/4" (12.1 cm) from the bottom of the light blue paper. Lightly draw a pencil line from the edge of the paper to the design. Do not draw the line on the maypole.
4. Carefully cut along the pencil line up to the design. Then cut around the maypole and continue cutting along the pencil line to the edge of the paper.
5. Follow directions on page 4 for making a standing pop-up card.
6. Match the folds for the inside and outside of the card before gluing. Then glue the maypole design to the inside of the purple paper. Be careful not to glue the pop-up section of the card.
7. Trace and cut out four girls and four boys. Glue the boys and girls around the streamers of the maypole.
8. Use crayons and scrap paper to decorate the card.
9. Write a May Day greeting on the inside of the card.

Greeting Cards for All Occasions ©1995 Fearon Teacher Aids

**boy
cut 1 of each color
red
green
blue
yellow**

**girl
cut 1 of each color
red
green
blue
yellow**

**bow
cut 7**

Children's Day

In Japan, the carp fish is a symbol of strength and power. On this holiday, originally called Boys' Festival, families flew one carp flag for each son. These "flags" are hollow. Air fills the fish bodies and they float like kites. Recently, Japan recreated this holiday to include both boys and girls. Flying kites is the major event of the day.

Materials

Pattern on page 81
Art Paper:
    Orange 5" x 18"
       (12.7 cm x 45.7 cm)
    Assorted scraps
Yarn 10" (25.4 cm)
Glitter
Chopstick
2 plastic eyes (optional)
Hole punch

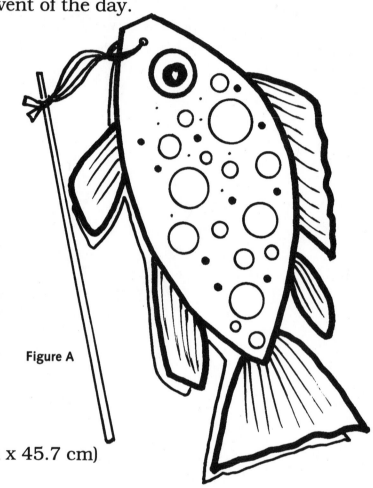

Figure A

Procedure

1. Fold orange 5" x 18" (12.7 cm x 45.7 cm) art paper in half.
2. Trace and cut out fish pattern from orange art paper. Do not cut through fold.
3. Trace and cut out various colors and sizes of circles from art paper scraps. Cut out enough circles to decorate both sides of the fish.
4. Glue eyes and multicolored circles on both sides of the fish.
5. Punch a hole near the fold of the fish. See Figure A.
6. Thread yarn through the hole and tie to chopstick.
7. Write message on the inside of the card.

Greeting Cards for All Occasions ©1995 Fearon Teacher Aids

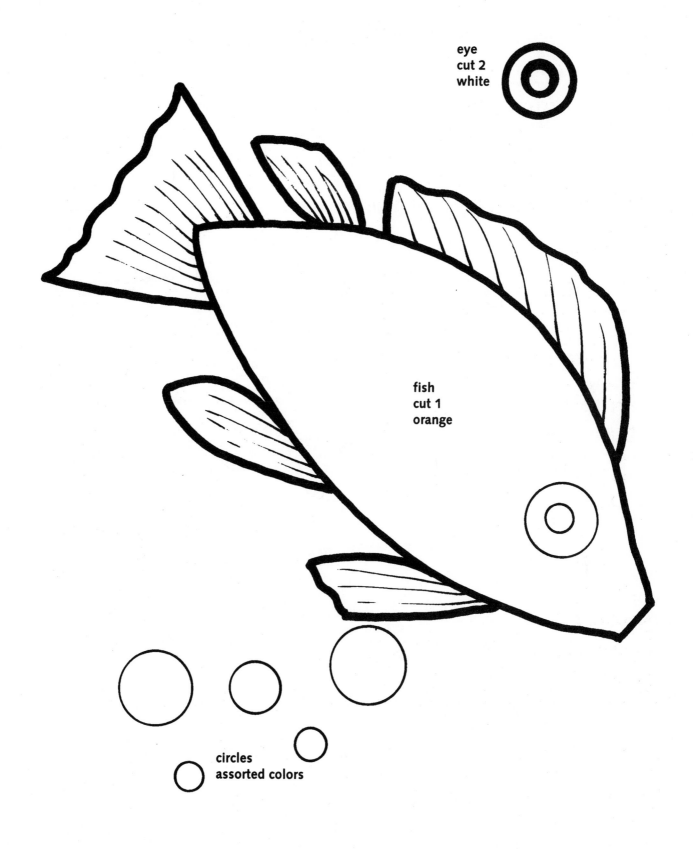

eye
cut 2
white

fish
cut 1
orange

circles
assorted colors

Cinco de Mayo (Boy)

This Mexican holiday commemorates the victory of the Mexican Army over French invasion forces at the city of Puebla on May 5, 1862. This holiday is also widely celebrated throughout the United States. Americans of Mexican ancestry express their pride in their heritage with parades, music, feasting, dancing, and traditional dress.

Materials

Pattern on page 83
Art Paper:
    Red 9" x 12"
        (22.9 cm x 30.5 cm)
    White 9" x 12"
        (22.9 cm x 30.5 cm)
    Assorted scraps
Mexican flag toothpick
    (optional)

Procedure

1. Reproduce pattern on page 83 on white 9" x 12" (22.9 cm x 30.5 cm) art paper.
2. Fold red and white 9" x 12" (22.9 cm x 30.5 cm) art paper in half.
3. Outline the pattern with a black felt pen. Then decorate with crayons or markers.
4. Carefully cut along the solid line from the edge of the paper, around the boy, to the other edge of the paper.
5. Follow directions on page 4 for making a standing pop-up card.
6. Match the folds for the inside and outside of the card before gluing. Then glue the boy design to the inside of the red paper. Be careful not to glue the pop-up section of the card.
7. Use crayons and scrap paper to decorate the card.
8. If desired, glue a toothpick Mexican flag in the boy's hand.

Greeting Cards for All Occasions ©1995 Fearon Teacher Aids

Cinco de Mayo (Girl)

Cinco de Mayo is a fiesta which means *feast* or *celebration* in Spanish. Celebrate Cinco de Mayo with Mexican foods, such as tacos, enchiladas, tamales, and chips and salsa.

Materials

Pattern on page 85
Art Paper:
    Purple 9" x 12"
      (22.9 cm x 30.5 cm)
    Yellow 9" x 12"
      (22.9 cm x 30.5 cm)
    Assorted scraps
Mexican flag toothpick
  (optional)

Procedure

1. Reproduce pattern on page 85 on yellow 9" x 12" (22.9 cm x 30.5 cm) art paper.
2. Fold purple and yellow 9" x 12" (22.9 cm x 30.5 cm) art papers in half.
3. Outline the pattern with a black felt pen. Then decorate with crayons or markers.
4. Carefully cut along the solid line from the edge of the paper, around the girl, to the other edge of the paper.
5. Follow directions on page 4 for making a standing pop-up card.
6. Match the folds for the inside and outside of the card before gluing. Then glue the girl design to the inside of the purple paper. Be careful not to glue the pop-up section of the card.
7. Use crayons and scrap paper to decorate the card.
8. If desired, glue a toothpick Mexican flag in the girl's hand.

Greeting Cards for All Occasions ©1995 Fearon Teacher Aids

Cinco de Mayo (Girl) **85**

Flower Basket

Many of our earliest memories of warmth, love, and strength come from our mothers. Thanks to Anna Jarvis of Grafton, West Virginia, Mother's Day became a national holiday of remembrance in 1911. On this day, many say thank you to their mothers with flowers, small gifts, and sometimes, breakfast in bed.

Materials

Pattern on page 87
Art Paper:
    White 9" x 12"
      (22.9 cm x 30.5 cm)
    White 4" x 4"
      (7.6 cm x 7.6 cm)
    Pink 4" x 4"
      (7.6 cm x 7.6 cm)
    Assorted scraps

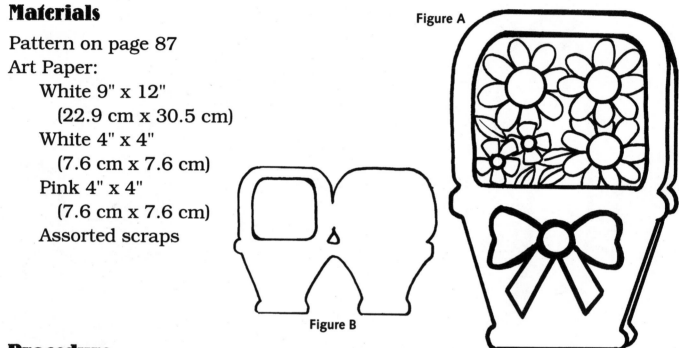

Figure A

Figure B

Procedure

1. Fold white 9" x 12" (22.9 cm x 30.5 cm) art paper in half. Then fold the paper in half again.
2. Place the basket pattern on page 87 on the fold. Trace around the pattern.
3. Carefully cut out the basket pattern. Do not cut the pattern where indicated.
4. Unfold the card and carefully cut out the center of the basket handle on the front of the card only. See Figure B.
5. Trace and cut out flowers from assorted scraps of art paper. Glue flowers to the inside of the card. See Figure A.
6. Trace and cut bow from pink art paper. Glue bow on front of the basket.
7. Print a Mother's Day message inside the card.

Greeting Cards for All Occasions ©1995 Fearon Teacher Aids

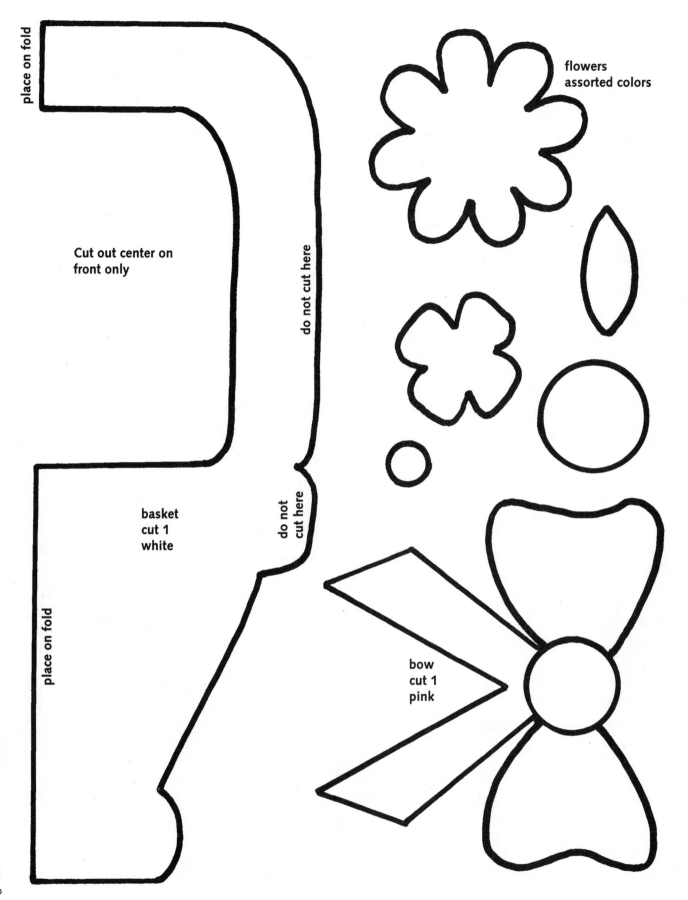

place on fold

Cut out center on
front only

do not cut here

basket
cut 1
white

do not
cut here

place on fold

flowers
assorted colors

bow
cut 1
pink

Flowerpot

Mother's Day is not only for mothers but it also includes grandmothers, too. Special gifts that your mother or grandmother would enjoy don't need to cost anything—weed the garden, wash the dishes, watch your brother or sister for an hour. Sometimes just giving your mother some quiet time can be a special gift, too.

Materials

Pattern on page 89
Art Paper:
    White 6" x 9"
      (15.2 cm x 22.9 cm)
    Purple 9" x 12"
      (22.9 cm x 30.5 cm)
    Yellow 2" x 3"
      (5.0 cm x 7.6 cm)
    Assorted scraps

Procedure

1. Fold purple 9" x 12" (22.9 cm x 30.5 cm) art paper in half.
2. Trace the pattern on page 89 on white 6" x 9" (15.2 cm x 22.9 cm) art paper.
3. Decorate the flowerpot with crayons or markers. Fold the flower in half.
4. Follow directions on page 4 for making a standing pop-up card.
5. Match the center folds for the flowerpot and the outside of the card before gluing. Then glue only the flowerpot (not the flower) to the inside of the purple paper.
6. Use crayons and scrap paper to decorate the background of the card.
7. Write a Mother's Day greeting on yellow 2" x 3" (5.0 cm x 7.6 cm) art paper. Glue message inside the card.

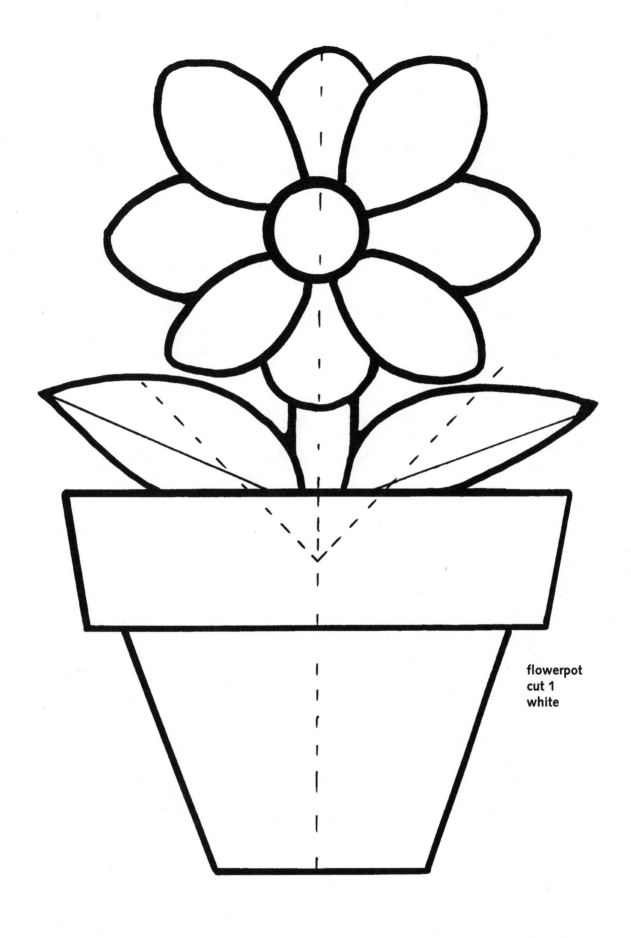

flowerpot
cut 1
white

BBQ

Father's Day is Dad's day off. Fathers' increasing involvement in parenting led Senator Margaret Chase Smith to create a new tradition in 1972: honoring fathers and their special contributions to the family. Father's Day, like Mother's Day, is now a national holiday.

Materials

Patterns on page 92
Art Paper:
    Brown 9" x 12"
      (22.9 cm x 30.5 cm)
    White 9" x 12"
      (22.9 cm x 30.5 cm)
    White 4" x 4"
      (7.6 cm x 7.6 cm)
    Red 6" x 9"
      (15.2 cm x 22.9 cm)
    Skin tone 6" x 6"
      (15.2 cm x 15.2 cm)
    Black scraps
White poster paint
Sponge 1" x 1" (2.5 cm x 2.5 cm)

Figure A

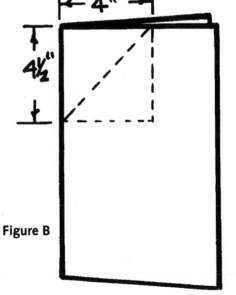

Figure B

Greeting Cards for All Occasions ©1995 Fearon Teacher Aids

Procedure

1. Fold both brown and white 9" x 12" (22.9 cm x 30.5 cm) art papers in half.
2. Measure and mark 4 1/2" (11.4 cm) down from the top of the brown art paper. Then measure and mark 4" (10.2 cm) from the fold. Draw a diagonal pencil line connecting the two marks. This is the fold line for the pop-up section. Fold along the pencil line, first, going to the right and then to the left. See Figure B.
3. Follow directions on page 4 for making a standing pop-up card.
4. Trace the patterns on page 92.
5. Glue the hat to the top of the head. Then use crayons to add details to the face.
6. Fold the head and hat in half with the face facing out. Glue the head to the center of the "v" fold on the brown art paper.
7. Glue the grill and three grill legs together. Then glue the grill below the "v" fold on the brown art paper. See Figure A.
8. Use white paint and a sponge to create smoke between the grill and the head. Glue the hands coming out of the smoke. Allow the paint to dry before handling.
9. Match the folds for the inside and outside of the card before gluing. Then glue the brown art paper to the inside of the white paper. Be careful not to glue the pop-up section of the card.
10. Glue the Father's Day greeting inside the card.

hat
cut 1
white

HAPPY, FATHER'S DAY

message
cut 1
white

head
cut 1
skin tone

grill
cut 1
red

place on fold

grill leg
cut 3
black

hand
cut 2
skin tone

Newspaper

Father's Day is an opportunity to honor your father with a special if not unusual gift. Some favorite choices for gifts are ties, socks, after shave, just to name a few. Encourage students to think of something unusual to give their fathers this year.

Materials

Patterns on page 94
Art Paper:

Brown 9" x 12" (22.9 cm x 30.5 cm)
Red 6" x 9" (15.2 cm x 22.9 cm)
White 6" x 9" (15.2 cm x 22.9 cm)
Skin tone 3" x 4" (7.6 cm x 10.2 cm)

Figure A

Procedure

1. Trace and cut out the patterns on page 94.
2. Fold brown 9" x 12" (22.9 cm x 30.5 cm) art paper in half.
3. Glue the chair, the newspaper, and the arms and legs together as shown in Figure A.
4. Decorate pattern pieces with crayons or markers.
5. Glue the chair to the inside fold of the brown art paper.
6. Write a Father's Day greeting on the newspaper.

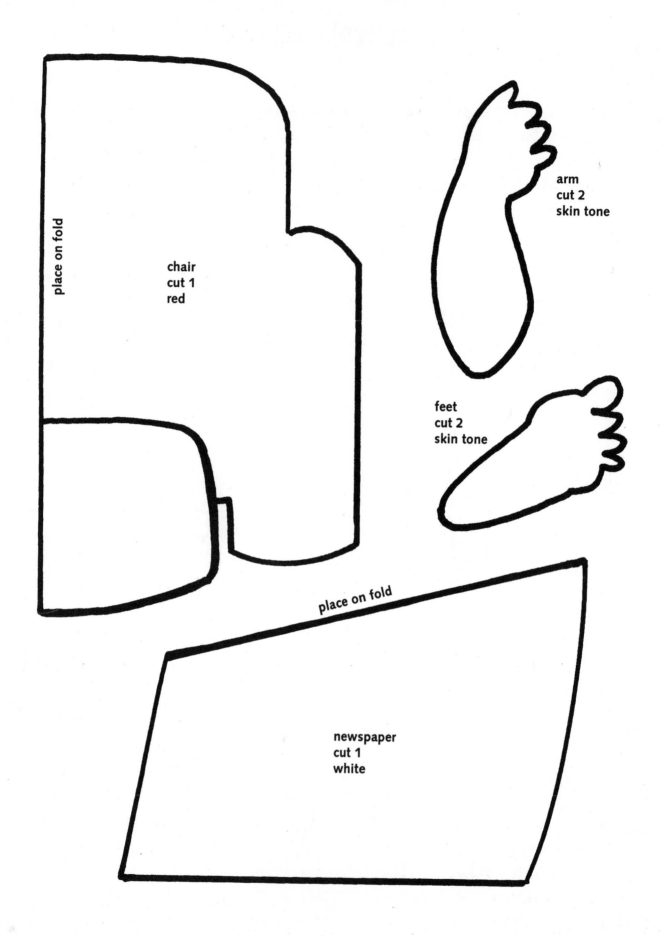

place on fold

chair
cut 1
red

arm
cut 2
skin tone

feet
cut 2
skin tone

place on fold

newspaper
cut 1
white

Greeting Cards for All Occasions ©1995 Fearon Teacher Aids

Canada Day

Happy Birthday, Canada! This holiday celebrates Canada's independence from Great Britain on July 1, 1867. The British colonies of New Brunswick, Nova Scotia, and the Province of Canada were finally united under one government. This is the most patriotic of Canada's holidays. Encourage students to think of creative ways to celebrate Canada's birthday.

Materials

Patterns on page 96
Art Paper:
  White 9" x 12"
    (22.9 cm x 30.5 cm)
  2 Red 9" x 12"
    (22.9 cm x 30.5 cm)
  Gray 2" x 4"
    (5.0 cm x 7.6 cm)

Procedure

1. Fold white 9" x 12" (22.9 cm x 30.5 cm) art paper in half.
2. Cut two red 2" x 9" (5.0 cm x 22.9 cm) strips. Trace leaves on red art paper.
3. Glue the red strips on the each side of the front of the card.
4. Follow directions on page 4 for making a standing pop-up card.
5. Match the folds for the maple leaf and the inside of the card before gluing. Then glue the large maple leaf on the fold of the white art paper. Be careful not to glue the pop-up section of the card.
6. Trace and cut out the banner on gray art paper. Glue the banner and small maple leaf on the front of the card.

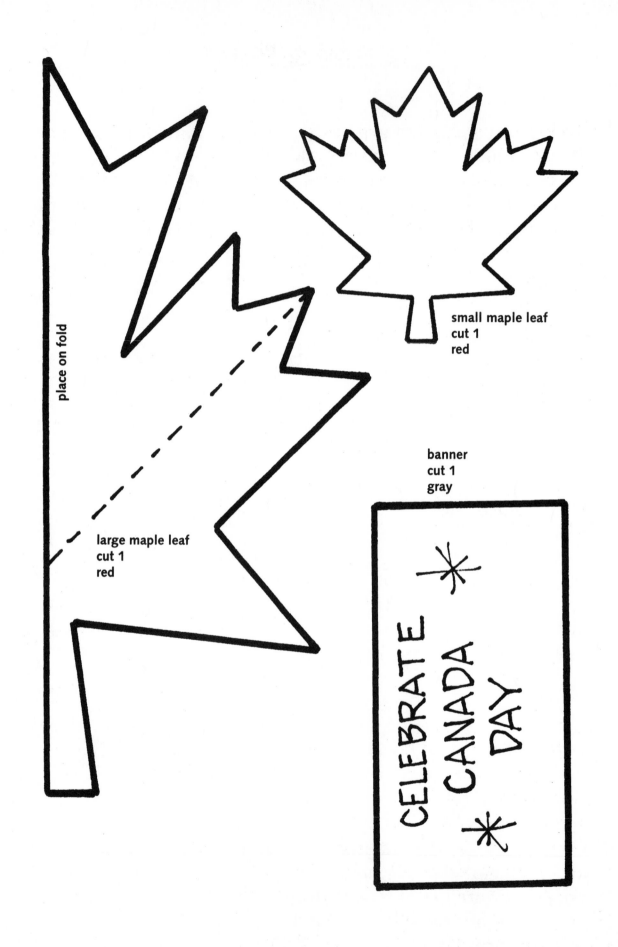

place on fold

large maple leaf
cut 1
red

small maple leaf
cut 1
red

banner
cut 1
gray

CELEBRATE
CANADA
DAY

Bald Eagle

The bald eagle was adopted as the national bird in 1782. This bird appears bald because its head and neck are covered with white feathers. The bald eagle was chosen because of its strength, dignity, and individuality. Benjamin Franklin thought that the turkey should have been chosen because it had better moral character and was more respectable. He claimed it was a true native of America. Ask students if they could choose an animal to represent the United States, what would it be and why.

Materials

Patterns on page 98
Art Paper:
    Blue 9" x 12"
      (22.9 cm x 30.5 cm)
    White 3 1/2" x 3 1/2"
      (8.9 cm x 8.9 cm)
    White 4" x 5"
      (10.2 cm x 12.7 cm)

Procedure

1. Fold blue 9" x 12" (22.9 cm x 30.5 cm) art paper in half.
2. Place the card in a horizontal position. Trace eagle on cover of blue art paper. The eagle's wings should appear along the fold.
3. Outline design with black felt pen.
4. Trace and cut out the separate shield on white 3 1/2" x 3 1/2" (8.9 cm x 8.9 cm) art paper. Glue the shield on the eagle.
5. Decorate the shield using red, white, and blue crayons or markers.
6. Write an Independence Day message on the 4" x 5" (10.2 cm x 12.7 cm) white art paper.
7. Glue the message on the inside of the card.

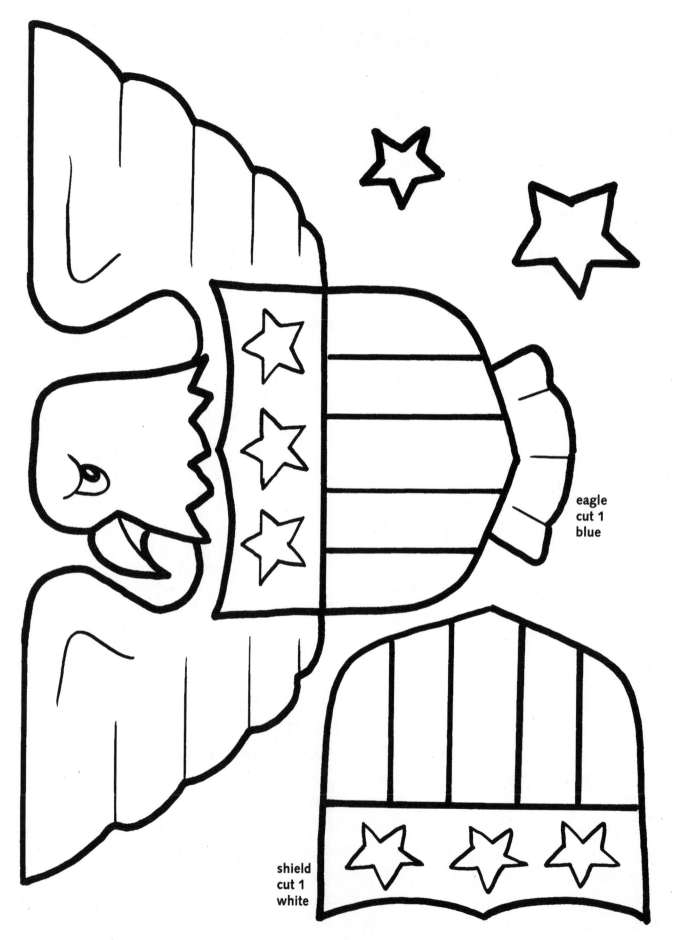

eagle
cut 1
blue

shield
cut 1
white

U.S. Independence Day (Bald Eagle)

Liberty Bell

Liberty means freedom. In July, 1776, the Liberty Bell rang out loud and clear. The Declaration of Independence, which declared the colonies' freedom from British rule, had been signed. The Liberty Bell weighs over 2,000 pounds and cost Pennsylvania $300. Unfortunately, the Liberty Bell can no longer ring. The bell was broken and cracked as it rang for the last time in 1835 to celebrate George Washington's birthday.

Materials

Patterns on page 100
Art Paper:
> White 9" x 12"
>> (22.9 cm x 30.5 cm)
> Red 6" x 9"
>> (15.2 cm x 22.9 cm)
> 3 Blue 1" x 6" strips
>> (2.5 cm x 15.2 cm)
> White scraps

Procedure

1. Fold white 9" x 12" (22.9 cm x 30.5 cm) art paper in half.
2. Trace and cut out bell pattern on red art paper.
3. Glue the three blue strips on the bell alternating red and blue stripes.
4. Cut out two stars and glue in place on the bell.
5. Draw a crack on the bell with a black felt pen. Glue the bell to the front of the card.
6. Print a message inside the card.

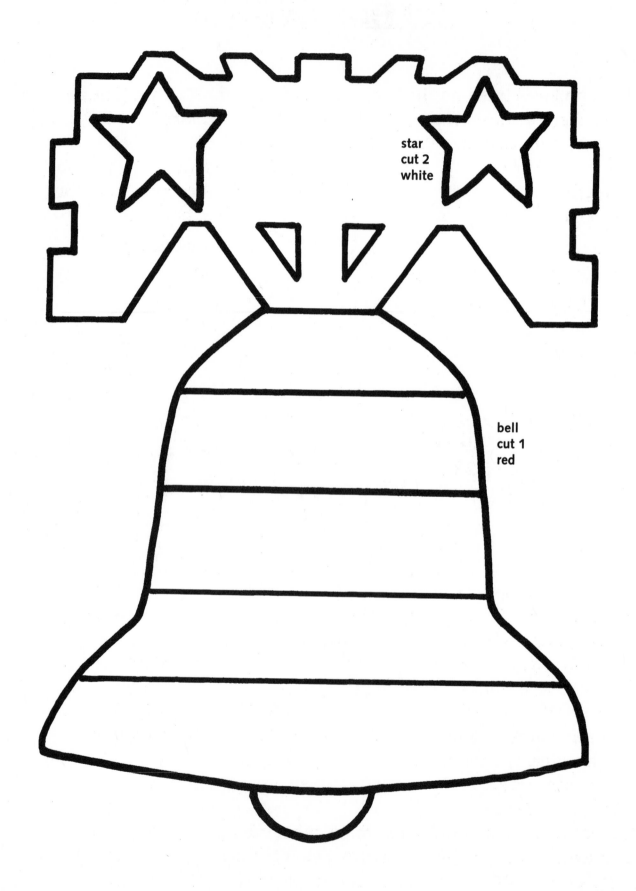

star
cut 2
white

bell
cut 1
red

Greeting Cards for All Occasions ©1995 Fearon Teacher Aids

Jack-in-the-Box

Everyone loves to be surprised on their birthday. What better way to surprise someone than with a jack-in-the-box. Encourage students to think of other birthday surprises they could send to a friend.

Materials

Patterns on page 102
Art Paper:
    Yellow 9" x 12"
      (22.9 cm x 30.5 cm)
    White 9" x 12"
      (22.9 cm x 30.5 cm)
    Pink 3 1/2" x 3 1/2"
      (8.9 cm x 8.9 cm)
    Orange 3 1/2" x 3 1/2"
      (8.9 cm x 8.9 cm)
Yarn 10" (25.4 cm)

Procedure

1. Fold yellow 9" x 12" (22.9 cm x 30.5 cm) art paper in half.
2. Reproduce the jack-in-the-box pattern including the arms on white art paper.
3. Decorate with crayons or markers. Outline the pattern with a black felt pen.
4. Cut out the jack-in-the-box. Follow directions on page 4 for making a standing pop-up card.
5. Match the center folds for the inside and outside of the card before gluing. Then glue only the box to the inside of the yellow paper. Be careful not to glue the pop-up section of the card.
6. Glue one arm directly to the yellow paper on each side of the jack-in-the-box.
7. Trace and cut out balloons. Write a birthday message on the balloons and glue balloons to the background of the card.
8. Glue yarn from the balloons to each hand of the jack-in-the-box. Fold the hands over the yarn pieces.

Greeting Cards for All Occasions ©1995 Fearon Teacher Aids

jack-in-the-box
cut 1
white

balloon
cut 1 of each
pink
orange

arm
cut 2
white

Cupcake

Ask students if they have ever made birthday wishes and then blown out the candles on the cake. If all the candles are blown out the wishes may come true.

Materials

Pattern on page 104
Art Paper:
    Light blue 9" x 12"
        (22.9 cm x 30.5 cm)
    White 9" x 12"
        (22.9 cm x 30.5 cm)
    Red scraps

Procedure

1. Fold light blue 9" x 12" (22.9 cm x 30.5 cm) art paper in half.
2. Reproduce the cupcake pattern on white 9" x 12" (22.9 cm x 30.5 cm) art paper.
3. Decorate with crayons or markers. Outline the pattern with black felt pen.
4. Cut out the cupcake. Follow directions on page 4 for making a standing pop-up card.
5. Match the center folds for the cupcake and outside of the card before gluing. Then glue only the cupcake to the inside of the light blue art paper. Be careful not to glue the pop-up section of the card.
6. Cut out and glue a red flame on top of the candle.
7. Write a birthday greeting inside the card.

candle flame
cut 1
red

cupcake
cut 1
white

Apple

Everyone enjoys getting a note of encouragement, even teachers and parents. Encourage students to give out apples of encouragement.

Materials

Pattern on page 106
Art Paper:
    Red 9" x 12" (22.9 cm x 30.5 cm)
    Green 3" x 4" (7.6 cm x 7.6 cm)
    White 3" x 4" (7.6 cm x 10.2 cm)
    Black scraps
Plastic eyes (optional)

Procedure

1. Fold red 9" x 12" (22.9 cm x 30.5 cm) art paper in half.
2. Trace and cut out apple pattern on red paper. Do not cut where indicated.
3. Trace and cut out eyes and leaf. Glue in place.
4. Decorate with crayons or markers.
5. Print greeting inside.

leaf
cut 1
green

eyeball
cut 2
white

eye
cut 2
black

place on fold

apple
cut 1
red

Greeting Cards for All Occasions ©1995 Fearon Teacher Aids

School House

The school house greeting card can be used as an invitation for an open house, parent/teacher conference, or school program. It would also be a nice card to send home with a good report card.

Materials

Pattern on page 108
Art Paper:
 Red 9" x 12"
  (22.9 cm x 30.5 cm)
 Black 3" x 3"
  (7.6 cm x 7.6 cm)
Aluminum foil 2" x 2"
  (5.0 cm x 5.0 cm)
Toothpick flag (optional)

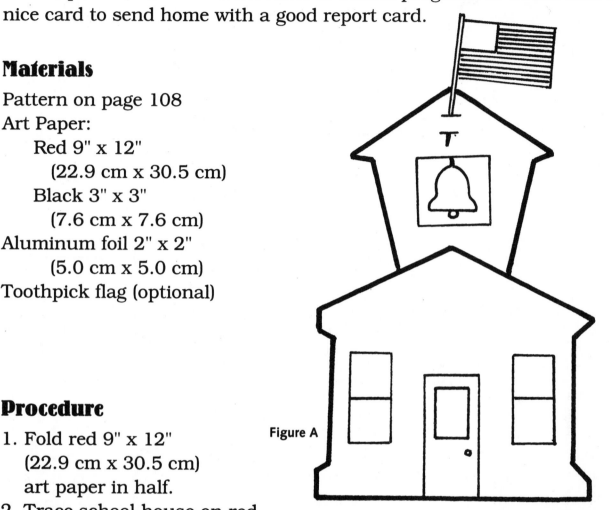

Figure A

Procedure

1. Fold red 9" x 12" (22.9 cm x 30.5 cm) art paper in half.
2. Trace school house on red art paper. Do not cut where indicated.
3. Trace and cut out bell from black art paper. Cover bell shape with aluminum foil.
4. Cut two black 1" x 2" (2.5 cm x 5.0 cm) rectangles for windows and one black 1" x 2 1/2" (2.5 cm x 6.3 cm) rectangle for the door. Glue the windows and door in place. See Figure A.
5. Print open house information on the inside of the card.
6. Cut square opening only in the cover of the school house. Glue foil covered bell inside the card. Cut slits for toothpick flag, if desired.

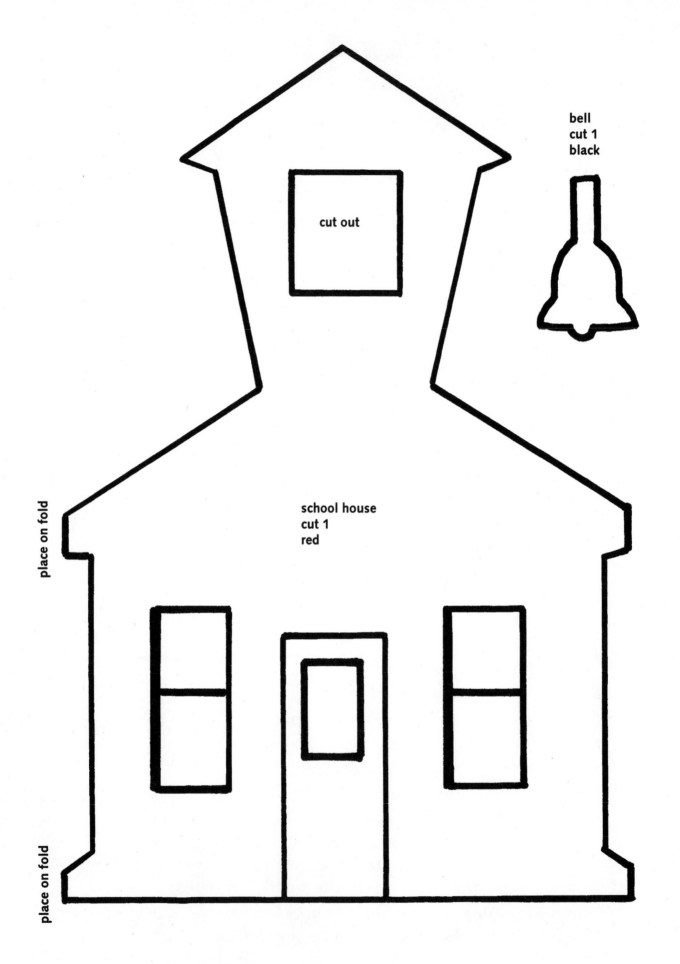

bell
cut 1
black

cut out

place on fold

school house
cut 1
red

place on fold

Greeting Cards for All Occasions ©1995 Fearon Teacher Aids